DESERT HIGHWAY

A Play in Two Acts
and One Interlude

by

J. B. PRIESTLEY

SAMUEL FRENCH LIMITED
LONDON

Copyright © 1944 by J.B. Priestley
All Rights Reserved

DESERT HIGHWAY is fully protected under the copyright laws of the British Commonwealth, including Canada, the United States of America, and all other countries of the Copyright Union. All rights, including professional and amateur stage productions, recitation, lecturing, public reading, motion picture, radio broadcasting, television and the rights of translation into foreign languages are strictly reserved.

ISBN 978-0-573-11654-4

www.samuelfrench.co.uk
www.samuelfrench.com

FOR AMATEUR PRODUCTION ENQUIRIES

UNITED KINGDOM AND WORLD EXCLUDING NORTH AMERICA

plays@samuelfrench.co.uk
020 7255 4302/01

Each title is subject to availability from Samuel French, depending upon country of performance.

CAUTION: Professional and amateur producers are hereby warned that *DESERT HIGHWAY* is subject to a licensing fee. Publication of this play does not imply availability for performance. Both amateurs and professionals considering a production are strongly advised to apply to the appropriate agent before starting rehearsals, advertising, or booking a theatre. A licensing fee must be paid whether the title is presented for charity or gain and whether or not admission is charged.

The Professional Rights in this play are controlled by United Agents LLP, 12-26 Lexington St, Soho, London W1F 0LE.

No one shall make any changes in this title for the purpose of production. No part of this book may be reproduced, stored in a retrieval system, or transmitted in any form, by any means, now known or yet to be invented, including mechanical, electronic, photocopying, recording, videotaping, or otherwise, without the prior written permission of the publisher. No one shall upload this title, or part of this title, to any social media websites.

The right of J.B. Priestley to be identified as author of this work has been asserted in accordance with Section 77 of the Copyright, Designs and Patents Act 1988.

DESERT HIGHWAY

Produced at the Playhouse, London, in March, 1944, with the following cast of characters :—

(In the order of their appearance.)

TROOPER ILTYDD HUGHES	W. Emlyn James.
TROOPER GEORGE WICK	Peter Tuddenham.
TROOPER ("KNOCKER") ELVIN	Stanley Rose.
CORPORAL PHILLIP DONNINGTON	John Wyse.
TROOPER HERBERT SHAW	George Cooper.
SERGEANT BEN JOSEPH	Stephen Murray.

The Members of the Cast are serving Soldiers.

Directed by MICHAEL MACOWAN.

Technical advice on R.A.C. procedure by Major Harry Barker, R.T.R.

Décor by George Ramon.

SYNOPSIS OF SCENES

ACT I.—During the present war. Evening.
Interval of ten minutes.

INTERLUDE.—The same place, about the year 703 B.C.
Interval of ten minutes.

ACT II.—During the present war. Next morning.

The Scene is a hollow near an old Highway in the Syrian Desert, where—it is assumed for the purpose of this play—a campaign is being fought.

NOTE BY THE AUTHOR

This play was specially written for the Army and has been presented to it as a small tribute from a soldier of the last war to the soldiers of this one.

Although it has some humour in it—or at least, I hope you will find it has it is essentially a serious play, because, after all, war is a very serious business. The central theme of the play is also to my mind, the central theme of our whole war effort.

The two Acts that take place during the present war need no explanation, but I must say something about the middle Act, which I have called an Interlude. Here you see the same place in the Syrian Desert over two thousand six hundred years ago. I chose this particular time because it was a time of confusion and war and suffering, like ours, when the powerful Assyrian Empire, which was really a vast military organisation not unlike Hitler's Germany, was invading and looting and burning its way throughout the Middle East, and also because this was the time of the great Hebrew prophets, such as Isaiah, whose words are still alive to-day. Many of you may find this part of the play strange and remote and therefore perhaps not very interesting, but I want you to try to see what I am getting at in this Interlude, if only because it sets the two modern scenes in relief, against the long perspective of world history, and, if it does nothing else, it reminds us that men have been fighting, wondering, suffering, hoping, for thousands of years, just as we are doing to-day. History shows us mankind as a long, long procession of brothers for ever losing and finding and losing again their essential brotherhood. It is our turn now to make a supreme effort to find that brotherhood, and this play is a small contribution to that great task. I hope you will enjoy it.

J. B. PRIESTLEY.

NOTES ON THE CHARACTERS

SERGEANT JOSEPH is a well-built, thoughtful Jew of the best type, aged about thirty. His ascendency over the other men is due to his personality rather than to his rank; he has no Jewish accent, but speaks as an ordinary London secondary schoolboy would speak. He is a sensitive follow, but very virile.

CORPORAL PHILLIP DONNINGTON is a public school and university man, also about thirty. He ought to have a commission but cannot be bothered and does not want any responsibility. Is the kind of educated man who wanders from job to job, and rather likes low company and probably drinks too much in civil life. Indifferent and cynical. Preferably of rather slight physique.

"KNOCKER" ELVIN is a Cockney of the Cockneys. Old enough to have fought in the last war. Old soldier. Does anything in civil life. Ought to be a sergeant at least but prefers to be a private. Physically and mentally, very tough. But temperamental.

HERBERT SHAW is a hefty, solemn West Riding working-class type, in his late twenties. Slow and stubborn. Speaks with marked Yorkshire accent.

ILTYDD HUGHES is a dark, quick Welshman, in his early thirties, very temperamental. Very Welsh in accent and manner and general outlook.

GEORGE WICK is a fresh-faced country lad, easily the baby of the party, with something very young and innocent and pleasantly foolish about him. About twenty. Preferably should speak with something like a Gloucestershire accent, but any not too marked rural accent will do, so long as it is not North-country or Welsh.

DESERT HIGHWAY

ACT I

The SCENE is a hollow near an old highway in the Syrian Desert. The setting can be more or less elaborate, according to the circumstances of production. These notes assume a full stage and ordinary theatrical equipment.

In the distance, nothing but sky can be seen.

In the foreground, running from R. to L., is a long low ridge of rocks and sand (see Ground Plan at the end of the book) of varying levels. These rocks can be sat upon, and also mounted at various points (as indicated in the script) to the ridge proper, the basis of which is a central rostrum with a ramp at either end leading down to stage level.

Prominent in the ridge, at L.C., is a piece of worn, carved stone, less than a foot high, suggesting a buried stone monument or idol of some kind. Near it, a hump of rock which is frequently used as a seat by some of the characters.

The total impression is that of a harsh desert.

At the opening of this Act there is a hard, bright evening light.

On the R., partially hidden, is a Grant tank. It is not necessary that the actors should be seen getting in or coming out of it, but it must be possible for them to enter and exit both above and below it.

On the L., down stage, is a small desert tent, the opening of which faces slightly up R., so that anybody going into the tent can leave the stage unseen by the audience.

Various equipment—blankets, ground sheets, etc., has already been brought out of the tank, suggesting that the men intend to spend the night there.

Other properties, and their positions, are described in the Property Plot.

All the men wear desert clothes, and though deeply sun-burned, look dusty, tired and short of sleep.

When the CURTAIN rises, HUGHES and WICK are kneeling to R. of the tent. HUGHES, R. of WICK, is holding open a sandbag while the latter fills it with a shovel from a pile of sand nearby.

HUGHES. So I said to myself—I said—" Iltydd Hughes," I said, " you are going to have bad luck this time," I said.

WICK. I don't believe you can tell if you're going to have bad luck.

HUGHES. Certainly you can tell—if you have the gift. My grandmother had the gift—she was *terrible*. So was my Uncle Thomas. *(He rises, and goes R. to the tank, selects a sandbag from the pile, and returns to WICK.)*

WICK (*placing the filled bag in front of the tent*). I've got an Uncle Thomas. (*He returns to* HUGHES, L.C.) Runs a baker's and confectioner's in Moreton-on-the-Marsh.

HUGHES (*holding open the fresh bag*). It's not a business I would care to be in—baking. Gets you up too early in the morning.

WICK (*busy filling the bag*). You have to get up early on a farm too. I was used to it.

HUGHES (*rather proudly*). I have worked on a farm. It belonged to my cousin—in Mid-Wales. I went there for my health when I was seventeen. "An outdoor life for you, my boy," they said. "Yes, an outdoor life." So I had an outdoor life. And now I'm having another outdoor life. (*He rises, and takes the sandbag to the tent, kneeling to set it in place.*

(WICK *rises, moves up the rocks to the rostrum, and looks round as if trying to see into the distance. He pauses, and then turns to* HUGHES.)

WICK. I say—Taffy—— (*He hesitates.*)

HUGHES (*rising to his feet*). Whatever you are going to say, Georgie—don't call me Taff. I don't like it. Hughes—or Mister Hughes as it often was in Civvy Street—or Iltydd—I don't mind. I don't care if you call me nothing at all. But not Taff. It sounds like Elvin—and I don't like the man. (*He turns up to the rock up* C.)

WICK. Okay, sorry.

HUGHES (*moving to* WICK *and sits on the edge below and to* L. *of* WICK). But you were going to ask me something, I think, Georgie—eh?

WICK (*dropping his voice—crouching*). That's right. But I was only going to ask—d'you think we're all right here?

HUGHES (*flustered*). All right here? Certainly we're all right here—I suppose. (*From dubiousness now to alarm.*) Why shouldn't we be all right? Nothing wrong with us, is there? The tank's broken down—temporarily, I suppose, quite temporarily—but we've plenty of rations and water—and we can have a nice little rest. All right? Certainly—we're all right.

WICK (*who catches the final tone of doubt*). Sergeant Joseph knows all about it, doesn't he?

HUGHES. Of course he does. He's one of the *very* best.

(*Enter* ELVIN R. *from below the tank. He carries a Bren gun box, and moves towards* L. WICK *climbs down to the stage to help him.*)

ELVIN (*boisterously, as they carry the box to* L.C.). Got the ol' tent up, eh? Good job your mother doesn't know about this little packet, Georgie. Fed up, mucked up, an' far from 'ome—that's us.

(*They put the gun box down* L.C., *just below the ledge of rock.*)

HUGHES (*indignantly*). Why do you talk to him like that?

(*He comes down from the ledge to* C. *of the stage* R. *of* WICK.)

ELVIN. What's the matter with you, Lloyd George?

HUGHES (*furiously*). I'm telling you, Knocker Elvin——

ELVIN (*angry now*). Don't call me Knocker. Only my chinas—like young Georgie 'ere—call me Knocker—see?—any little Welsh mucker can't call me Knocker. As soon as the Sarge tells me oo's in this bleedin' party, I says, " For Gord's sake leave Taffy out," I says—" 'cos 'e'll bring a packet, 'e will. First thing yer knows, Sarge," I says, " something'll break down or get mucked up, just mark my bleedin' words," I says. An' 'ere we are.

VOICE OF SERGEANT JOSEPH (*from inside the tank*). Knocker!

ELVIN (*calling*). Yes, Sergeant? (*He moves to* R.C.)

VOICE OF JOSEPH (*sharply*). We're hungry. Get cracking.

ELVIN (*calling*). Ready when you are, Sergeant. (*To* WICK.) 'Ere, give me a 'and, Georgie.

(WICK *crosses* R.)

(*They go out* R *behind the tank.* HUGHES *watches them go with marked distaste, and messes about, tidying up the equipment for a moment, placing water-cans in the tent.* DONNINGTON *enters, as from the tank.*)

DONNINGTON. That's the quietest radio set I ever listened to. (*Sitting on the low rock* R.C.). You can't even catch a crooner.

(*He produces a packet of cigarettes.* HUGHES *comes nearer and stares at them.* DONNINGTON *looks up and sees him.*)

All right, you'll be giving yourself eyestrain in a minute. Here you are.

(*He tosses him a cigarette. They light up.*)

HUGHES. I am very much obliged to you, Corporal Donnington. Very much obliged to you.

DONNINGTON (*ironical, but not unfriendly*). Don't mention it, Trooper Hughes, don't mention it.

HUGHES. I have sometimes thought it would be much better not to smoke at all—(*He sits on the lower ledge* C. *stage to* L. *of* DONNINGTON) like young Georgie—because then if I didn't smoke at all, I wouldn't miss it if I had nothing to smoke—if you see what I mean, Corporal.

DONNINGTON. No difficulty at all in following that thought. I feel the same about whisky. If you'd never had it, you'd never miss it. And anyhow, I could never really afford it.

Born too late. My father had all the luck—except when he produced me. Ever have any trouble with your father, Hughes ?

HUGHES (*rather startled*). Oh—no—no trouble at all. He was very nice, my father. But he's dead now.

DONNINGTON. So is mine, only he doesn't know it.

HUGHES (*startled again*). But—if he was dead——

DONNINGTON. No, don't thrash it out. Leave it.

HUGHES (*solemnly*). No, I see now what you mean, Corporal. You know, I have often thought you are a bitter man.

DONNINGTON. Yes, yes—a cynical type.

HUGHES. I think you have had some trouble with a woman.

DONNINGTON. I think so too. Matter of fact, I saw her last week.

HUGHES (*astounded*). You saw her ? But how could you see her ?

DONNINGTON. Captain Fawcett—I knew him slightly before the war—let me look at an old copy of the " Tatler " he had. She was in. Doing something nice and fancy for the Red Cross —for our gallant boys overseas. You're one of our gallant boys overseas, you know. How d'you feel ?

HUGHES. I should like very much to be at home hearing about it on the wircless.

DONNINGTON. Let me get back and I won't listen to it on the wireless. I've had enough listening on *this* wireless—and hearing nothing. Which means that nobody knows where we are, and we don't know where anybody else is.

HUGHES. The recce planes can spot us.

DONNINGTON. Yes, but whose recce planes ? The wrong lot may spot us first. However, it's no use worrying about that.

HUGHES. No, I was saying to young Georgie that we have a good man, one of the very best, in Sergeant Joseph.

DONNINGTON. Yes, that's our only bit of luck. It might have been that fool Stanners, or that belly-ache—Nash. Ben Joseph's a bit too solemn for my taste, but he does know his stuff.

HUGHES. Certainly, one of the very best. And yet I heard Elvin calling him a teapot.

DONNINGTON. That's all right. Knocker's a real Cockney and uses the old rhyming slang. " Teapot " is short for " teapot lid," and that's rhyming slang for " Yid." In other words, Knocker's only saying in his elaborate way that our sergeant is a Jew. That's why he takes this war so seriously, because he's a Jew. I might do the same myself if I were a Jew.

HUGHES. There are some Jews in my town, but they weren't like the sergeant—very different they are.

DONNINGTON. Well, there are all kinds of Jews, y'know—fat and thin, rich and poor, noisy ones and quiet ones, some in the front line, some in the Black Market—like the rest of us. Only, perhaps, a bit tougher.

HUGHES (*seriously*). It is a great pleasure to me to listen to an educated man like yourself, Corporal. Cambridge no doubt ?

DONNINGTON. Oxford, if we must mention it.

HUGHES (*moving nearer to* DONNINGTON). My cousin Aneurin is studying at the University of Wales—at Bangor.

DONNINGTON. He's probably in " Itma " by this time. Were you with us when Ben Joseph—he was only a corporal then—won the middleweight championship of the two armoured divisions for us ?

HUGHES. No, but I heard of it. Both Elvin and Shaw have told me all about it.

DONNINGTON. They wanted to give him a job in Cairo, just to keep him boxing, but he turned it down. In fact, he said he'd never do any more fighting—except the military kind. He got a bit solemn after that. But he's all right.

(*Enter* SHAW, *as from the tank. He is very dirty.*)

SHAW (*indicating the tank*). Bloody 'opeless. (*He sits down heavily on a box in front of the tank.*)

DONNINGTON (*mockingly*). Our 'Erbert from Ossett—our sweet little ray of sunshine !

SHAW. Well, if it's bloody 'opeless, what's good o' saying it isn't ? It'll take lads in t'workshops all ther time to get her goin' again.

HUGHES (*rises and moves down* L.C.). What's happened to her ?

SHAW. Everything's 'appened. To start wi', steering-box is a proper muck-up. There was something wrong wi' yon tank when we took 'er over. I said so from t'start, didn't I, Corporal ?

DONNINGTON. Certainly, Herbert. Ever since I've known you, you've been passing on bad news—and enjoying it. Are they all like you in Ossett ?

SHAW (*grimly*). Ah don't know—but Ah wish Ah wor back to find out. An' Ah could ha' been reserved if Ah'd gone t'engine-room at Ackroyd's—same as me father said—but o' course Ah took no notice.

DONNINGTON. Is your father like you, Herbert ?

SHAW (*seriously*). Oh no, me father's a more serious sort o' chap. An' me grandfather's more serious still.

DONNINGTON. He must be carved out of granite.

SHAW. He's a big man at t'chapel, me grandfather is.

HUGHES. So was mine.

SHAW. Ay, but it's diff'rent up ahr way.

DONNINGTON. If ever I get out of this, I must have a look at Ossett.

Shaw. Ay, but we're not aht of it yet. Sergeant's trying t'wireless again.

(Hughes *sits on the lowest ledge of rock below the " monument."*)

Donnington. I couldn't get a thing out of it.

Shaw. Eee—Ah'm 'ungry.

Donnington (*rising*). We'll be eating in a minute, but don't think too much about it. We'll have to go easy on the rations.

Shaw (*aghast*). What for ?

Donnington. Because we're stuck here and can't get away, and it may be a few days before anybody finds us. So work that out, Herbert. (*Climbing to the top of the ramp.*)

(Elvin *and* Wick *now appear with food and tea, from behind the tank, and place the food on the Bren gun box,* L.C. *The others get ready to feed.* Shaw *moves to* R.C. Donnington *walks down the ramp towards* L. Elvin *begins dishing out the food, throughout the following dialogue. After* Wick *has put the food down, he sits below the Bren gun box.*)

Elvin. Well, 'ere it is, chummies, what there is of it. An' don't blame me if yer 'ear it rattle inside, 'cos the Sarge tells me to cut it down—see ? An' yer can use yer common about that, Yorky, an' stop lookin' as if it's my muckin' fault we're abaht two hundred flamin' long miles from the Quarter-bloke an' another two hundred from the nearest Naffy.

(*As* Shaw *replies,* Donnington *moves from the ramp to* L.C. *He tastes the tea and then sits down by the tent.*)

Shaw (*gloomily*). Proper muck-up. (*He hands his mug to* Elvin.)

Elvin. Go orn, Yorky. (*Filling the mug and handing it to* Shaw.) You blokes ought to 'ave 'ad some o' the scran we 'ad in the last war, when there wasn't this Lord Whoozit makin' up a nice tin 'o this an' a nice tin o' that for the boys (Wick *hands down the tin with the food*) when they gives yer biscuit an' bully, bully an' biscuit till yer teeth was wurn dahn an' yer bleedin' at the gums—iron rations 'alf the muckin' time, an' iron rations was iron all right them days. You blokes is livin' in Lyons Corner 'Ouse now only yer don't know it.

(Shaw *takes his mug and food to* R., *below the tank.*)

Wick. I went to one of them once. There was a band playing. (*He sits below the Bren gun box, facing* Donnington.)

Elvin. I'll bet there was, Georgie boy. (*As* Hughes *gets his mug and spoon from the tent and kneels in front of the tea bucket to get his tea.*) An' some nice little bints to dish out the chow, eh ? Well, take yer mind right off it, Georgie. (*Calling.*) It's up, Sergeant. (*To the others, now sitting round.*) Just take a butcher's at it first.

HUGHES. What butcher's? (*Still kneeling by the bucket.*)

ELVIN. Yer so ignerant I can't talk to yer, Taffy. I meantersay, take a nice long look at it first—'cos it's not polite to start eatin' before the sergeant's 'ere, an' what's more important—yer'll 'ave to spin it out—see?

(SERGEANT JOSEPH *enters, as from the tank, looking rather tired and concerned.*)

'Ere y'are, Sergeant. All dished up an' waitin' for the word o' command.

(HUGHES *returns to the seat on the lower ledge* L.C.)

An' I've told these blokes we got to spin it out a bit.

JOSEPH (*taking his portion*). That's right, Knocker. (*Looking at his portion.*) Here, you've given me too much. Take some of this back. I'm not very hungry. (*He sits on the rock* R.C.)

SHAW (*crossing to* C.). Not 'ungry! I could eat a horse. (*He hands* ELVIN *his mess-tin.*)

ELVIN (*refilling tin and returning to* R. *of the gun box*). Betchercould, Yorky. But yer couldn't eat ol' Lizzie there—— (*He points to the tank.*) That's where we bin mugs, see. We oughter stuck to 'orses.

WICK. But you haven't ever eaten horse, have you, Knocker?

ELVIN (*leaning against the rocks,* C.). Eaten 'orse! Gahrblimey, I've eaten dozens o' bleedin' 'orses—wiv chips an' cabbage.

HUGHES. You must think, man, we believe anything you tell us.

ELVIN (*contemptuously*). Oh—turn it up, Taffy. (*Handing him a mess-tin from the box.*) Yer ignerant—never bin anywhere—never seen anything—whazza-use o' talkin' to you.

(HUGHES *takes his mess-tin.*)

DONNINGTON (*to* HUGHES). Knocker's not kidding you. I've eaten horse. It's like beef—only coarser and a bit sweeter——

ELVIN. 'At's right. (*He climbs on* C. *of the rostrum and sits, putting his tea mug beside him.*) The corporal knows. Eddicated man, see. 'E's 'ad 'orse. So've I, dozens of 'em. (*Eating.*) Ol' Derby winners, some of 'em. An' dahn at ol' Ma Pellini's, just off the Mile End Road—yer could 'ave jockeys on toast wiv 'em.

(*Throughout this dialogue they are eating, and dishing out the second course, etc.*)

WICK (*lying on his left elbow*). I'd like to go to this Ma Pellini's you're always talking about, Knocker.

ELVIN. Take yer there soon as we're back in Civvy Street, me ol' china. Best caff in the East End, Ma Pellini's is. Serve yer anything there—any blinkin' thing yer fancy—if yer know 'ow to ask for it. One ol' bloke—keeps a furniture shop back o' Stepney Green—used to go there re'lar an' plenty o' nicker, see—an' this ol' bloke 'ad to 'ave sheep's 'ead every time. Taffy, it'd 'a' frightened yer blinkin' life aht ter see 'im there every time with 'is sheep's 'ead front of 'im——

HUGHES (*rising to it, angrily*). Why should it have frightened me to see him with a sheep's head?

ELVIN (*guffawing*). Yer might ha' thought it one o' your relations——

HUGHES (*furiously, rising to his feet*). I'll knock your face in, you Knocker, you——

(ELVIN *comes down and faces* HUGHES *ready for a scrap, he sits again as* JOSEPH *speaks.*)

SHAW. Steady on, lads.

ELVIN (*contemptuously*). Ow—'im! 'E couldn't——

JOSEPH (*sharply*). Drop it, Knocker. And don't let's have any more of it. And don't you listen to his nonsense, Hughes. He's only trying to make you lose your temper.

HUGHES. I am a very quiet man, Sergeant—and always known to be not at all quarrelsome—but—if he starts . . .

JOSEPH. All right. Just stay quiet, that's all. You too, Knocker.

ELVIN (*quite good-humouredly*). Every time, Sarge.

(HUGHES *refills his mug and sits on the rock* L.)

JOSEPH (*looking round at them, slowly*). You're not in camp now. You're out in the desert—and a long way out in it. A lot of things could happen to us, the spot we're in now. Even if there was any sense in it—and there isn't—we haven't energy to waste on meaningless quarrels. So we'd all better be quiet men for a day or two.

(*He produces a Service notebook and begins writing in it, rather slowly.* ELVIN *climbs to the top of the rostrum,* C.)

DONNINGTON (*after a pause*). Writing a report?

JOSEPH. Yes. If we're lost here—as we seem to be just now —I want to show them that it wasn't our fault. We went the way we were told. We haven't got to the rendezvous because of this breakdown, of course, but if the others had gone the right way, we wouldn't be clean out of touch as we are now. I think they went wrong this side of Asmar Oasis.

SHAW. Same 'ere, Sergeant. Ah said so at time, didn't Ah?

(ELVIN *lights a cigarette and lies full length on top of the rostrum.*)

DONNINGTON. That's Stanners and Nash (*He rises and moves to the rock* R.C., L. *of* JOSEPH)—knowing it all, as usual.
JOSEPH. When did you first complain to me about the steering, Shaw?
SHAW. About middle o' t'morning. Ah said then there wor summat up with 'er.
JOSEPH (*writing*). Yes, I remember. Well, I'll get this report straight as far as it goes.
(*They are smoking now, after their meal. After a pause,* DONNINGTON *begins, slowly and rather bitterly.*)
DONNINGTON. I could do a nice report on this set-up. (*He sits on the ledge of rock,* C.) A nice sweet little report.
ELVIN. I'll buy it, Corporal. (*He moves his head only to* DONNINGTON.)
DONNINGTON (*slowly, as before*). Lost—in the Syrian Desert—a few thousand miles from home—six bloody fools and a broken-down tank. The rest of the division having taken the wrong turning. But only after about a thousand million idiots took the wrong turning.
WICK. I don't see that, Corporal. Who's this thousand million you're talking about?
ELVIN (*rising and resting on his elbow*). All the blokes 'at goes an' 'as a flamin' war all over again—see? Use your loaf, Georgie boy. Carry on, Corp. (*Lying down as before.*)
DONNINGTON (*as if enumerating*). In charge—Sergeant Ben Joseph—Military Medal—of London—formerly skilled craftsman employed by the Scientific Instrument Company—and if he'd had any sense he'd have been with 'em yet, as he easily could have been.
JOSEPH (*looking up*). All right—that's enough about me. You're next, Corporal Philip Donnington——
DONNINGTON. Also of London—formerly journalist, advertising agent's tout, publicity man for three restaurants and two night clubs——
ELVIN (*rising on to his elbow, looking at* DONNINGTON). Blimey—I knew you'd seen a bit o' life, Corp. Two night clubs! Cor lumme—an' pickin' up some nice lolly too, I'll be bound. Wotdger want ter go an' get yerself landed in this packet for?
DONNINGTON. I told you, I'm one of six bloody fools. I ought to have been talking about you for the B.B.C. (*mimicking a broadcaster*) "I want to talk to you to-night about our brave fellows in the Middle East——"
SHAW. I'd tell 'em summat if they'd let me 'ave a go.
ELVIN. They'd take you for a bleedin' comedian, Yorky. 'Appidrome, that's you.
SHAW (*glumly*). Happy-nothin'.
DONNINGTON. Then there's Trooper Knocker Elvin—also of

London—old sweat knows what it's like and yet hasn't the sense to keep out of it again——

ELVIN. That's me. No common—as per usual.

DONNINGTON. And what were you before you joined up?

ELVIN (*evasively*). I did this an' that. I got arahnd an' enjoyed meself.

DONNINGTON. Trooper Herbert Shaw—of Ossett—formerly employed, I believe, in the engine-room of a textile mill. Must join up. Must come out here. What for?

SHAW. Ah knaw, Ah knaw. Ah might ha' been poppin' into t'Are an' 'Ounds now for a pint, afore doin' a bit o' courtin'——

WICK (*grinning*). Which one would it have been to-night, Herbert? (*He rolls over onto his stomach.*)

JOSEPH (*smiling, looking up*) Has he got more than one girl?

WICK. He's got two haven't you, Herbert—and he can't decide which he wants. There's Nelly, the thin one in the tobacco shop—and Olive, the fat one at the confectioner's——

SHAW. Nay, she's not fat. Ah never said she wor fat. Ah only said she wasn't so thin as Nelly. Ay, an' Ah think it 'ud ha' been Olive's turn to-night. Aaa! (*He sighs.*) Ah 'adn't sense Ah wor born wi'.

(WICK *turns back on his left elbow.*)

DONNINGTON. Trooper Iltydd Hughes—of some unpronounceable place in Wales . . .

HUGHES. "Heolgerrigpeullgaerllangyfelach."

DONNINGTON. . . . where I don't know quite what he did——

HUGHES (*eagerly*). Worked for my uncle—builder and contractor—reserved occupation really—and very very nice business, growing all the time, it was, before the war. I quite agree with you, Corporal—no sense in us at all to be here.

DONNINGTON. Then Trooper George Wick—(WICK *sits up, turns and faces* DONNINGTON) just off the farm and really just out of the egg—from Little Muddlem——

WICK (*seriously, correcting him*). Long Micklem. I keep on telling you, Corporal, but you won't get it right. It's Long Micklem. And we've got the best farm there. It's been hundreds of years in our family. One day I'll have it. (*He lies back, his hands behind his head.*)

HUGHES. Touch wood.

(ELVIN *slides off the rostrum to the stage.*)

ELVIN. Garn—'e don't need to touch no wood, Georgie don't. (*He moves to* WICK, *turning to* HUGHES.) Super*stu*tious —that's what you are, Taffy. Super*stu*tious, see? An' it all comes of bleedin' ignerance—now then——

ACT I] DESERT HIGHWAY 15

HUGHES (*rising again*). Ignorant yourself, you loud-mouthed Cockney, you——
DONNINGTON (*with authority, sharply*). Turn it up, you two! I haven't finished my nice little report yet.
(ELVIN *sits, also* HUGHES.)
JOSEPH (*looking up from his writing*). It seemed to me to peter out even worse than my report.
DONNINGTON. Now wait. The aforementioned B.F.'s now sitting in the desert may be discovered there by the enemy. If they are, either they will be killed—(WICK *rises to his left elbow*) which will be the end of them—or they'll be taken prisoner, to live a degraded sort of existence for a few years before being returned to a country that's forgotten them. If, on the other hand, they are found by their own side, they will be required almost immediately to take part in similar idiotic expeditions. But if these six are found by neither side——
JOSEPH (*quietly but decidedly*). All right, Phil, you needn't go into that.
ELVIN (*who has been thinking this over*). Cheerful sort o' chummie, you are, Corp'ral, aren't yer? My bleedin' oath, you are!
SHAW. Ah agree wi' every word 'e said. An' Ah feel better nah 'e's said it. Me an' the Corporal thinks alike.
JOSEPH (*now coming into the talk*). No you don't. Not really. But you both enjoy making the worst of things. (*He rises.*)
WICK. Herbert does. Grumbles like hell all the time, an' makes me feel low sometimes.
JOSEPH (*taking charge now, moves* C., *to the* L. *of* DONNINGTON). Now let's have another look at this soldiering business. We're all fools for being here, eh?
HUGHES. Certainly we are, Sergeant Joseph. No doubt of that whatever.
ELVIN. If I 'eard my ticket was waiting for me down at the base—desert or no bleedin' desert—I'd start runnin' for it now.
JOSEPH. You would, Knocker, eh?
ELVIN. I would, Sar'n't. Gone with the flamin' wind—that'ud be me.
JOSEPH. And yet I happen to know, Knocker, that you were offered a permanent job down at the base, on account of your age and service, and that you turned it down—to come up here.
ELVIN (*apologetically*). That's diff'rent. If I'm goin' ter soldier, then I'm goin' ter soldier—see—an' no char-wallah stuff at the base—I like to be up the line with the real boys—see. I done it before—an' I can do it again—never mind if I'm in a desert or on a bleedin' iceberg. But show me me ticket——
JOSEPH (*loudly, affectionately*). Go on, you old liar. If I showed you your ticket now—you wouldn't have it.

ELVIN. You couldn't run fast enough to take it away from me——

JOSEPH. I see. And if they'd sent transport for you, then you'd just climb in, say good-bye, and leave us here to get on without you, eh?

ELVIN (*embarrassed by this argument*). Oh—well—'ave a bit o' common, Sar'n't—they wouldn't send transport for me an' not for the rest of you—so it just couldn't 'appen. But I say——

DONNINGTON (*breaking in*). It doesn't matter what you say, Knocker. We know it's all talk. You needn't have been here at all. But then—you've got it badly—you can't keep away from soldiering—you're practically barmy—so you don't count. If there is an argument, you can be left out. But what *is* the argument, Ben?

JOSEPH (*squatting* C.). Well, you say—and they all agree with you—that we're fools to be here. Right?

DONNINGTON. Right.

JOSEPH. And I say—let's take a look at it. What's the alternative to fighting, to being fools out here? Well, we might have all packed up. In nineteen-forty say, when they expected us to. I don't know where some of you would have been then—working for the Nazi bosses probably—but I know that, being a Jew, I'd have been in a concentration camp—that is, if they'd taken me alive—which they wouldn't have done——

SHAW (*indignantly. He rises from the box* R.). Nah then, steady on a minute, Sergeant. They wouldn't ha' got me workin' for any bloody Nazis. We don't like them sort o' folk up i' Yorkshire.

HUGHES (*excitedly, rising to down* L.C.). If England had given in, Wales would have gone on fighting by herself—under Lloyd George perhaps——

ELVIN (*with great emphasis—rising*). 'Ere, 'alf a minute, you blokes—'oo d'yer think you are? What abaht good ol' London? Why—if yer'd all packed it up—ol' Winston 'ad only to come down the Mile End Road an' give the word—an' we'd ha' fought 'em wiv bleedin' bottles. Pack up! 'Oo the 'ell ever talked o' packing it up at any time—— (*He moves* L.C.)

DONNINGTON. Nobody did. And the sergeant knows it. He's only arguing.

(SHAW *sits on the box* R. HUGHES *sits, down* L. ELVIN *sits on the ledge of rock* L. *of the Bren gun box.*)

We had to fight. So what?

JOSEPH (*rising*). Well, if we had to fight, somebody had to leave home, go out, and do the fighting. But it needn't have been us. We're the fools, the mugs. The smart boys—we'll say—are all still at home. Georgie here might have been still on his farm, Shaw in a factory, Corporal Donnington might have been at the Ministry of Information——

ELVIN. Cripes! Excuse my glove, Corporal! (*He offers his hand—business of shaking hands in the air.*)

JOSEPH. And then you wouldn't have been fools out here, would you? You'd have been all right. Not a bad war at all. Go on, just imagine yourselves doing it—with all the rest of the chaps out here, of course. Sitting at home, listening to the wireless at night. Fine, eh?

ELVIN (*slowly*). I dunno, Sar'n't—it doesn't sound so 'ot ter me. Of course, if yer could get yer ticket good an' proper—that 'ud be diff'rent——

WICK. No, I don't think I'd like that, Sergeant. Not with all the other chaps away. It isn't the same at home.

JOSEPH. Phil?

DONNINGTON. Oh—I get the idea. The argument's plain enough. It would have been worse still if we'd packed up and refused to fight. All right. But we wouldn't have been happy if we'd stayed at home and let other fellows do the fighting for us. Therefore, we're not fools to be here.

JOSEPH (*sits on the rocks below the rostrum*). Right. And what's your answer to that?

DONNINGTON (*rising, and speaking with growing emphasis*). My answer is—we're all fools—fools or crooks. What sort of a world is it that offers a man these alternatives? Either fight or be whipped. Either sit on the desert or stay at home eating your damned heart out? Either behave like a fool or behave like a crook. What a choice! What a world! (*He turns to the tank.*)

HUGHES. Now you are talking, Corporal Donnington. I agree with you.

JOSEPH. Go on, Phil.

DONNINGTON (*faces the rest*). What's the use? You must see it for yourself. This isn't a life, this isn't a civilization—it's nothing but a hell on earth. Women and young children trapped and screaming in blazing ruins. Chaps going mad in open boats. Whole cities burning. Millions and millions of young men throwing hot lead at each other, high in the sky or down in holes in the ground. Whole countries dying of starvation. Hundreds of thousands of factories turning out nothing but planes and tanks and guns, when people want food and clothes and houses. No people getting on with their real lives. Nothing but war, war, war—torture, starvation and mass murder. And what the hell's the use of arguing about who started it? The point is—it shouldn't have been there to start. Fools! I tell you, we're all bloody madmen, the whole stinking human race. (*He sits on the ledge of rock* R.C.)

ELVIN. Gahr-lumme, yer've said something this time, Corp.

HUGHES (*rising*). He's right—quite right indeed, I tell you. My uncle says the very same thing. We are all mad, he says. In the chapel he says it too—for my uncle is a very fine preacher too.

SHAW. Corporal's not doing too bad at it either.

JOSEPH (*quietly*). That all, Phil?

DONNINGTON. No, it isn't, and I might as well finish now that I've got going. We've made it a hell on earth, and for all I can see, it's going to stay like that. We're all fighting for a better world, are we? Yes, they're all telling us that now. I've heard 'em. And they make me laugh. They make me laugh because I don't want to cry, that's all. Better world my foot! Who's telling us we're fighting for a better world? All the old crooks who helped to get us into this mess, and who go round telling the people how brave they are, instead of getting down on their knees and asking to be forgiven because they got 'em into this filthy mess. We had one great war, which knocked off about ten million men. Did anybody learn anything? Not one goddamned thing, except how to make faster planes, bigger bombs and heavier tanks. And now we're in another war, worse still. And is anybody learning anything? Not a thing. You listen to 'em. You read what they say. For all I can see, in another twenty years, we'll all be at it again, worse than ever. Listen—and don't try to be funny, because I can't take it just now. I quarrelled with a girl once—the only one I ever really cared about—simply because she wouldn't give me a child. Well, now I know she was right. (*He rises.*) I wouldn't bring a deaf-blind monkey into such a world. Let it rot.

(DONNINGTON *walks away to the ramp, above the tank, to hide his feelings. The others are silent, watching him go.*)

JOSEPH (*quietly*). Phil?

DONNINGTON (*over his shoulder*). Okay, Ben. I'm all right.

(*He goes out* R.)

WICK (*after a pause, sitting up and clasping his knees*). I didn't understand all that.

ELVIN. That's 'cos yer too young, Georgie boy. What did you make o' that little packet, Sar'n't?

JOSEPH (*putting his notebook away*). Doesn't make much odds what I thought of it, Knocker. You see, I'm different from the rest of you.

ELVIN. What—'cos yer got three stripes?

JOSEPH. No, of course not. But, you see, I'm a Jew.

HUGHES. Why should that make any difference?

JOSEPH. We've a history that goes back a long way. And a lot has happened to us. Mostly unpleasant. What's happening now has happened before to us—this is the worst because

ACT I]   DESERT HIGHWAY   19

it's the most thorough and ruthless—but we've had it before. That makes the difference.

SHAW. Ah dare say—but Ah don't quite see what you're getting at, Sergeant.

HUGHES. I don't either.

JOSEPH. If there's time to explain later on, I will. (*He rises, moves to the ramp and faces the tank.*) And it's just possible we might have a lot of time on our hands just now. (*Calling.*) Phil?

DONNINGTON (*off, from the tank*). Yes?

JOSEPH (*calling*). Try the wireless again.

DONNINGTON (*off, calling*). I am doing. But I can't get anything.

JOSEPH (*calling*). Keep on with it. (*To the others.*) Get cleaned up here, boys. (*He moves to the rock* R.C.) And don't be too long about it, because it'll be dark fairly soon—(WICK *collects up mess-tins and cups from* C. *and* L.C.) and I want you two, Shaw and Hughes, to see to the guns and check the ammo —and you two, Elvin and Wick (HUGHES *brings mugs and tins from* R.C. *to* WICK *at* C.) check the rations and water. There is water over there, isn't there, Knocker?

(WICK *exits* R., *with some of the mugs and tins.*)

ELVIN (*at* C.). 'At's ri', Sar'n't—I 'ad a dekko at it when we first come. Not so ruddy much, there isn't, an' what there is there's dark an' crawlin'—looks more like maggoty potted meat.

JOSEPH. We can chlorinate it and boil it.

ELVIN. Yer could make bleedin' rissoles out of it.

JOSEPH (*moving to the ramp, then facing them*). Bring some in when you've cleared up.

(HUGHES *exits down* R. *with the tea-bucket.*)

I'm going to see if we can't get some sense out of that wireless. And all of you keep a sharp look-out for planes. It's not too late yet for one to be passing—either one of ours or one of theirs.

(*He goes off behind the tank.* ELVIN *and* SHAW *clear up.*)

SHAW. Water. Yer never think about water till yer in one o' these God-forsaken 'oles. (*He takes a mess-tin to the box* C.) At 'ome yer just turn tap on an' there it is—much as yer want.

(WICK *re-enters above the tank, and collects* ELVIN'S *cup from the rostrum.* SHAW *moves to* R.C.)

ELVIN (*following* SHAW *to* R.C.). Yus, an' what's better still, Yorky—yer can step out to the nearest boozer—an' say " Pint o' bitter "—an' she pulls the ol' 'andle—an' there y'are.

(HUGHES *re-enters down* R. *with a tommy-gun. He sits on the box* R., *to clean it, as* SHAW *and* ELVIN *move* R., *above the tank.*)

An' I'll bet there's some blokes grumblin' 'cos the price 'as gone up or there's a fly in it—Strewth!

(ELVIN *and* SHAW *exit above the tank* R.)

WICK (*sitting* L. *of* HUGHES). First time I went home on leave our farm was nearly flooded out. It was just after there'd been a lot of snow and then it had all melted, and all the low fields and the bottom of the road were under water.

(*Enter* ELVIN *from down* R. *He stands looking at* WICK.)

I come home that time late at night and there was a bright moon, and all the water was glittering—it looked fine.

ELVIN. There oughter bin some rockets an' a band playin'.

HUGHES. A mile up the hill from where I live, in the woods, there's a wonderful waterfall. Everybody comes to see it. You hear it roaring long before you see it, and in the spring the woods are full of bluebells.

(SHAW *re-enters* R., *above the tank*.)

Sometimes we took our suppers up there, and then came back through the woods—singing all together...

(SHAW *moves on to the ramp* R.C., *and looks across the desert*.)

When you come to stay with us, Georgie, after the war, we will go an' see the waterfall.

ELVIN. Nah wait a minute, Taff. First thing Georgie does when they let 'im off the farm (WICK *rises very disturbed*) is to come an' see me an' the ol' trouble-an' strife an' a few o' my ol' chinas—proper ruddy characters—that 'e's already 'eard tell of from me—see? 'At's right, isn't it, Georgie?

WICK. Well—— (*He stops short, and looks so serious that the others stare at him*.)

ELVIN. Wazzamatta, Georgie boy?

WICK (*turning away deeply disturbed*). I don't know. (*He moves to* C. *with his back to* ELVIN, *shaking his head*.)

ELVIN (*with gruff concern, moving to* WICK, C.). Take it easy, china, take it easy. 'At's a boy. Time you get back 'ome, your 'ol' man an' your brother'll 'ave piled so much nicker out o' that farm, all you'll 'ave to do is to bite the end off yer cigars an' strike matches—when me an' Yorky an' Taff is wonderin' 'ow to scrape a few bob together.

SHAW. An' Ah'll bet that's right an' all.

WICK (*gravely*). I'll fetch that water, shall I? (*He moves to the tent for the water-can*.)

ELVIN (*cheerfully*). That's right. Feel better when you come back, you'll see. Only keep yer 'and out o' that water. It might bite yer.

(WICK *exits* L., *over the ramp. The others watch him go, exchanging significant glances.*)

SHAW (*quietly*). What's up with 'im?

(ELVIN *moves up to the rostrum.*)

ELVIN. I dunno. But don't get it inter yer 'ead the poor little bleeder's windy—'cos 'e isn't.

HUGHES. He did it once before when we were talking about after the war.

SHAW. Did what?

HUGHES. He stopped suddenly—and wouldn't say any more—and then he walked away—shaking his head.

ELVIN (*standing* C.). 'At's why I let 'im go fer the water—see? Gives 'im something to do by 'imself—so's 'e can say, " 'Ere I am, Mother—in the bleedin' desert—all oky-doky " or—or whatever 'e wants to say to 'er. 'E's a good boy to 'is mother, young Georgie is.

(SHAW *moves on to the rostrum* R.C.)

Not like me. I was a proper bastard to my ol' woman—till I come 'ome on leaf—last war it was—wiv my mind made up to give the ol' girl a good time—an' then it was too late—they'd just taken 'er into the East London Horspital——

SHAW (*who is looking intently across* L.). Hey! Knocker!

ELVIN. Wazzamatter?

SHAW. Plane.

(*All three move up on to the rostrum and stare at the sky out* L. *We cannot hear anything yet, but they can.*)

HUGHES. I can't see it, but I can hear it.

SHAW. It's comin' this way an' all. (*Turning to call.*) Sergeant, Sergeant! Plane! (*He moves a little nearer* C., *on the rostrum.*)

ELVIN (*going to* L. *to shout*). Hey, Georgie! Plane! Plane!

(JOSEPH *and* DONNINGTON *come hurrying on, above the tank. They carry field-glasses, and at once look in the direction indicated by the others. We can now hear the plane distantly but steadily approaching.*)

JOSEPH. I told you one of our planes would spot us.

DONNINGTON. I suppose it is one of ours?

HUGHES. Must be.

JOSEPH (*watching through the field-glasses*). Wait a minute! I don't recognize this one! May be one of the new American—no! It's one of theirs—*take cover!*

ELVIN (*shouting to* L.). Hey, Georgie! Down, boy, down!

JOSEPH (*turning* R.). Come on—take cover!

(*They hurry off behind the tank.* ELVIN *is last to leave, and now we hear the plane coming fast and low. A burst of machine-gun fire off* L. *and then, with the plane immediately above, another burst of machine-gun fire aimed at the tank, etc. The whole incident should be staged as realistically and dramatically as possible. We hear the plane going away.* JOSEPH *re-enters and mounts to the top of the rostrum,* C., *standing as high as possible, watching the plane go, through his glasses. The others emerge, rather cautiously, with the rather forced jocularity of men coming out of a crisis.* DONNINGTON *and* HUGHES *are on the ramp at* R.C. ELVIN *and* SHAW *are down* R.)

ELVIN. Well, that bleeder took a nice crack at us all right, all right.

JOSEPH (*still looking*). He's not turning. Wants to get back. Lucky for us it'll be dark soon.

SHAW (*down* R. *in front of the tank*). If Ah'd 'ad gun out, Ah'd 'ave leathered yon chap. Ah put a burst right into one, time we wor near t' Canal. Saucy mucker!

ELVIN. 'Ow's young Georgie doin', Sar'n't?

(JOSEPH *looks off* L., *with the glasses.*)

Did 'e get down all right—same as I told 'im?

JOSEPH. Yes, he's down. Taking his time about getting up too. Thinks he might be coming back at him. Better tell him it's all right now. Here! (*He breaks off, and looks harder.*) He's been hit. Get the first-aid box.

(DONNINGTON *dashes to the tent* L.)

Hughes, you come with me. Knocker, get some water going. You other two, stay here—put some blankets in the tent. Come on, Hughes.

(*He and* HUGHES *race off* L.)

ELVIN (*dazed for a moment*). Georgie! Christ!

(DONNINGTON *comes out of the tent with a first-aid box.*)

DONNINGTON (*quietly*). Get going, Knocker. (*Moving to him* C.) You can curse it all afterwards. (*He goes up a little, back to the audience.*)

(ELVIN *exits behind the tank.*)

SHAW. It may be nowt after all. (*He takes a blanket from the mud-guard of the tank and crosses* L.) Ah've seen chaps knocked flat an' it's turned out to be nowt but a scratch.

(*He goes into the tent with the blanket.*)

DONNINGTON (*slowly, turning to face the tent*). I hope the kid's all right. But I have a feeling he isn't.

(*The light begins to fade slowly.*)

SHAW (*reappearing*). Seems to me, Corporal, (*moving near to* DONNINGTON) you've got some fairly 'orrible sorts o' thoughts an' feelings in that 'ead o' yours, if what you give us in that speech o' yours was a fair sample. An' Ah'm not so sure you're not right an' all. It's a mad monkey-'ouse we're in, all right.

DONNINGTON. You've noticed it too, have you ? (*Opening the gun-box.*)

SHAW (L.C.). Course Ah 'ave. Couple o' chaps come in a plane—they don't knaw us an' we don't knaw them—an' they're miles from 'ome an' so are we—they pump some lead out—an' dahn goes poor little George Wick. Seems to me if chaps at top can't arrange it better nor this, it'ud be cheaper to shoot them instead o' shooting each other.

DONNINGTON (*crossing down* R., *for the parts of the tommy-gun*). Wouldn't make any difference. It isn't just the chaps at the top—as you call them. (*He returns* C. *with gun parts.*) What's wrong goes all through.

(*They pack the gun in the box as he speaks.*)

Nobody learns anything, and nobody wants to. We're all barmy somewhere inside. The Nazis and Fascists and Japs are worse than we are, but we're barmy too.

SHAW. Well, Ah don't knaw. Ah don't feel barmy.

(ELVIN *re-enters* R., *below the tank, and goes up on the rostrum, looking off* L., *for* WICK'S *return.*)

Corporal says we're all barmy.

(SHAW *and* DONNINGTON *exit with box down* R.)

ELVIN. I've 'eard 'im before. (*Looking out* L.)

(DONNINGTON *and* SHAW *re-enter and join* ELVIN *on the rostrum.*)

Can't see 'em coming.

DONNINGTON. I expect they're putting a dressing on him. (*He gazes off* L. *from the rostrum.*)

ELVIN. I got the water goin'. Can't do no more 'ere. Might as well go an' give 'em a 'and wiv 'im, eh, Corp ?

DONNINGTON. All right, Knocker.

(ELVIN *hurries out* L. DONNINGTON *moves towards the idol.*)

SHAW (*moving on to the ramp*). Yer'd think to 'ear Knocker talk, 'e'd no more 'eart in 'im than that there stone, but Ah tell yer—he's right fond o' young Georgie, is Knocker. Do owt for 'im.

DONNINGTON (*after a pause, sitting on the hump* L. *of the idol*). What do you call those two girls of yours in Ossett ?

SHAW. One's Nellie—and t'other's Olive. (*He sits on the rostrum* R.C.)

DONNINGTON. Nellie and Olive. And I'll bet they're both going out with chaps to-night.

SHAW (*heartily*). An' Ah'll bet they are an' all. Me sister told me as much t'last letter she wrote. They've got t'Air Force round there, so they're off out wi' t'Air Force.

DONNINGTON. And don't you care?

SHAW. Well, Ah'd sooner think o' summat else than what's going on there—but Ah can't grumble, can Ah? Ah mean to say—if Ah can't make me mind whether it's Nellie Ah want or Olive, Ah can't blame 'em if they go aht wi' t'Air Force. Not that they mightn't do that onny way. An Ah must say if a nice-lookin' Waaf come along to-night, Ah might ha' one or two ideas o' me own.

DONNINGTON (*with mock gravity*). Yes, you might. But I have a feeling that a nice-looking Waaf—or a nice-looking anybody else—won't come along to-night. (*He quotes with slight over-emphasis.*)

> " White in the moon the long road lies,
> The moon stands blank above ;
> White in the moon the long road lies
> That leads me from my love.
> Still hangs the hedge without a gust
> Still, still the shadows stay ;
> My feet upon the moonlit dust
> Pursue the ceaseless way "

SHAW. That's poetry, in'it?

DONNINGTON. That's poetry.

SHAW. We 'ad poetry at school, but I thought nowt on it then 'an Ah've never bothered with it since. But that's all right, what you said. You mun gi' me that bit again sometime, Corporal. (*He repeats carefully.*) " White in t'moon—t'long road lies—'at leads me from me love." Ah see what t'chap's gettin' at there.

(*The lighting has faded, except for moonlight, and a red glow in the sky.*)

DONNINGTON. They'd better hurry up. It'll be dark soon.

SHAW. Ay, it's light one minute 'ere an' dark next. (*He rises.*) Ah reckon nowt o' that. Ah like it gradual same as it is at 'ome. (*He moves to* C. *of the rostrum.*)

DONNINGTON. They're bringing him back. Nothing more we can do here, is there?

SHAW (*staring about him*). Nowt as I can see. (*He sits* R. *of the idol.*) 'Ere, Corporal, Ah wonder what this 'ere stone is.

(*He indicates the top of the stone monument prominent in the background.*)

(*Both men look at it.*)

DONNINGTON. Probably some old stone monument—or what's left of it—buried deep in the sand. I believe this is an old desert road. Thousands of years ago men were travelling this way, and probably some of them often spent the night in this very place. I don't suppose they were very different from what we are. They were on the road too, far from home, wondering what was happening back there, wondering what it's all about, laughing and cursing and crying out and dying.

SHAW. Ay, 'appen this stone could tell a lot if it could talk.

DONNINGTON. Yes. But could it tell us what we want to know ? Could it tell us why we hurt each other and hurt ourselves and why there's something inside us that cries out in rage and shame at this misery and then dies before we do ?

SHAW. Nah, steady on, Corporal. (*He rises and looks across the desert.*) Things is bad enough without talkin' so peculiar. You give me the bloody creeps once already. 'Ere they are. (*He moves off the rostrum to down* L.C.)

(DONNINGTON *has risen.* SHAW *moves* L., *as* JOSEPH, HUGHES *and* ELVIN *enter slowly* L., *carrying* WICK, *who is obviously very badly wounded.* ELVIN *steps over the ramp* L., *and takes* WICK'S *head as* SHAW *takes his legs from* JOSEPH *and* HUGHES. *They carry him into the tent.* JOSEPH *comes over the ramp, followed by* HUGHES.)

JOSEPH (*quietly*). Straight into the tent with him. You stay with him first, Hughes, then we'll relieve you. Now steady—take it easy.

DONNINGTON (*quietly, coming down* C.). How is he, Ben ?

JOSEPH. Pretty bad. Had to give him morphia.

ELVIN (*to* HUGHES, *inside the tent*). I'll get a bit o' shut-eye now, Taff, then yer can wake me up soon as you like—an' I'll watch 'im. (*He comes from the tent, goes over to the tank and prepares the bed.*)

JOSEPH. All right, Knocker, you get some sleep now. You'd better get down too, Shaw.

SHAW. All right, Sergeant. (*He crosses to below the tent and sets a blanket, preparing to get ready for sleep by the tank.*)

JOSEPH. I'm going to have another go at that wireless, Phil. It wasn't so good before—with nobody knowing where we are—but now that plane has spotted us, and with young Wick on our hands, we've got to send a message somehow.

(*He moves towards the tank to stop just short of it.* DONNINGTON *follows him.*)

DONNINGTON. Well, I'm no radio expert, but there's one little dodge they showed me on that course that I'd like to try. (*As they move.*) How is the kid?
JOSEPH (*moving*). Too bad to last long out here.

(*He exits above the tank, followed by* DONNINGTON. *The red glow in the sky has faded. It is much darker, but the rostrum is moonlit.* SHAW *and* ELVIN *have got their blankets and are now preparing to sleep. They talk very quietly as they get down.*)

SHAW (*wrapping his blanket around himself*). 'Eard what the Sergeant said about young Georgie?
ELVIN (*doing the same*). I 'eard. But I needn't tell 'im ter tell me. I've seen too many blokes knocked aht not ter know that poor kid's bleedin' bad.
SHAW. That's right. (*He lies down under the ground-sheet.*)
ELVIN. 'E didn't know 'em when they got to 'im. Cryin' out an' talkin' to 'is mother an' brother, 'e was. I call it a perishin' ruddy shame. It's always them good kids that gets it. (*He is down with* SHAW *under the ground-sheet until the* CURTAIN.)
SHAW (*drowsily*). Ay—remember young Kitchen—an' that young Durham lad who played the mouth-organ——
ELVIN (*drowsily*). I can remember 'undreds of 'em—this war—last war—India an' Palestine too—'undreds of 'em—'undreds of 'em——
SHAW (*after a pause, drowsily*). Corporal says chaps 'as been travelling this way for thousands of years—thousands of years, 'e says——
ELVIN (*almost asleep*). 'Undreds of 'em—yers—'undreds of 'em——
SHAW (*almost asleep*). Thousands o' years—this same desert —thousands o' years . . .

(*They are now asleep. The stage is almost dark. Only the shaft of moonlight falls around the idol. Then a faint greenish misty glow in the sky begins to appear.*)

The CURTAIN *falls slowly.*

(INTERLUDE)

The SCENE *is the same, but now it is* 703 B.C.
Where the tank was, R., *is now a large rock. Down* L., *in place of the tent, there are various bundles and a large box* L.C., *to suggest this is a caravan on the move. It is full daylight. The characters are more or less the same, but of course their accents are less marked.* ELVIN, SHAW, HUGHES *and* WICK *are of indeterminate Near Eastern nationality—or of various nationalities, but more or less alike because their trade, as caravanners,*

has made them alike. The three older men wear beards, only
WICK is smooth-faced. They wear dusty rough patched clothes.
DONNINGTON is different, for he is now an Egyptian scribe—
smooth, clean-shaven, neat, dressed in a white linen tunic or
something of the kind. JOSEPH is a shepherd from Judah and
is bearded—dark and roughly dressed. The idol is newer
looking, and rises higher out of the ground than in Act I.

When the CURTAIN rises, HUGHES is alone on the stage, kneeling
before the idol, his back towards the R. entrance. He remains
prostrated before the idol, motionless for several moments, and
then ELVIN enters R. from above the rock, where all R. entrances
are made throughout, with the exception of SHAW'S and WICK'S
first entrance. ELVIN mounts the rock ledge at about R.C., to
behind HUGHES, and gives him a kick.

ELVIN. Get up.
HUGHES (*turning angrily*). Fool! (*But he scrambles to his feet.*) You may have angered the god.
ELVIN (*contemptuously*) God! That's no god. (*To the top of the rostrum* C.) You'll pray and sacrifice to anything. I told the overseer at Damascus that most of our trouble came from you, and that it was the last caravan I'd take with you——
HUGHES. That *you'd* take! Who made you the leader? I'm as good as you.
ELVIN. Oh no, you're not. I was travelling the desert when your mother was still wiping you—if she ever did wipe you.
HUGHES. We four are equal—two for the camels, two for the asses—and only the Egyptian is above us.
ELVIN. And who is it that the Egyptian asks for advice about the weather and the roads? He comes to me. He's promised me a job if I want it—when we reach Memphis.
HUGHES. We shall never reach Memphis—you'll see.
ELVIN. Oh—stop croaking! (*He moves down the ramp a pace or two* R.)
HUGHES. Besides, the Egyptians are all liars. (*To the top of the rostrum,* C.)
ELVIN (*turning to face* HUGHES). Oh—yes, the Egyptians are all liars. And why? Because you once lost a piece of silver to two black sorcerers at Tanis. You'd make anybody into a liar, you would, just because you'll believe anything. Praying to that! (*He points to the idol.*) Who is he, anyway?
HUGHES (*forcing* ELVIN *down the ramp away from the idol*). He may be the little god of this part of the desert.

(ELVIN *backs down on to the stage and sits on the rock* R.C.)

ELVIN. I don't give a fig for him. He's nobody. Hasn't even a name. If you'd had any sense, when we were up North, you'd have offered something to that old Hittite god—Teshub—

old Teshub riding on his bull—lord of the weather. Only time I gave him a miss, we lost half a caravan between here and Damascus. Remember that time, up North, when we looked into the gardens—and all the women were doing their annual weep—tearing their hair, shrieking and wailing, cutting themselves with sharp knives—while the fat eunuchs of Ashtoreth went walking round and round——?

(HUGHES *sits on the ledge of the ramp to the* R. *of* ELVIN.)

HUGHES. One of them saw us and cursed us. And then we lost five camels.

ELVIN. We'd have lost 'em anyhow.

(*Enter* SHAW R., *below the rock, carrying a bundle. He is followed by* WICK.)

SHAW (*crossing* L.). The Egyptian is still talking to the captain of the soldiers.

WICK. And the soldiers are preparing to go. (*He moves up* L.C., *on the ramp and looks about.*)

ELVIN. Are they coming our way?

SHAW (*putting his bundle down, below the boxes, kneeling by it*). I don't know. The Egyptian told us to wait.

WICK (*looking down at* SHAW). I want to get away from here Why can't we go?

SHAW. Take it easy. I keep telling him he'll never do for caravan work unless he can take it easy.

ELVIN. That's right, young one. Said the same to you myself.

WICK. It was my father's idea that I should make this journey. (*Sitting on the hump* R. *of the idol.*) I wanted to be a metal worker, like my uncle.

ELVIN. And stick in one place all your life?

WICK. Why not?

SHAW (*rising and moving round above the boxes as he speaks*). Well, you stay in a city, you build up a business, and then what —there's an invasion, the city's sacked, and either you're slit up or dragged off into slavery. I lost two brothers that way.

HUGHES (*sitting up*). And I lost my father and mother—and three of my father's brothers—and my sister was taken to Nineveh——

ELVIN. So that's who you were looking for, that time we went to Nineveh—your sister, eh?

HUGHES (*rises*). Yes, I went looking for my sister.

SHAW. Well, that wasn't your sister I saw you with. (*He sits on the box* L.C.)

(HUGHES *moves a little* R.)

WICK. I wish we'd been going to Nineveh. I should like to see it once.

HUGHES (*moving up on the ramp* R. *of* WICK). Beats them all, in my opinion, just as a place to see. You never saw such temples, parks and gardens. Wonderful. You could sit under the almond blossom in the gardens and smell the lilies, and watch the lions—hundreds and hundreds of lions they have there. (*To* ELVIN.) Haven't they?

ELVIN (*moving down, and round in a half circle to face the others*). Yes, but I liked the women—never mind the lions. All the people in the world are there at Nineveh. Every colour, shape and size. Streets crowded, inns packed out. Costs you plenty too—but it's fun while it lasts. Mind, I wouldn't live there—no fear.

WICK. Why?

ELVIN. You've got to be too careful. Do anything wrong—say a word too many—and they're on to you. They're cruel hard devils, the Assyrians. No, if I'm going to leave the road and stay anywhere, give me Egypt.

HUGHES (*jeeringly, sitting on the rostrum* C.). He thinks the Egyptians will offer him a job at Memphis.

ELVIN (*truculently*). Well, why not? (*He goes on to the ramp, facing* HUGHES *at* R.C.) Listen, there are chaps no better than me that have gone a long way in Egypt. And living's cheap, and you can get plenty of good beer. You're safe, too, in Egypt —you can risk raising a family—not like up here and along the coast, where before you know where you are—the town's burning, the invaders are in, and you're running for your life.

SHAW (*rising to up* L.C.). Yes, that's what it's like up here, but, if you ask me, it's the same everywhere else now—Egypt or anywhere. (*He sits below the idol.*) Nobody's safe any more. You heard what that old man said who came out of the cave back there—when was it, day before yesterday. He said the gods were angry and so the world was coming to an end.

WICK. But he was mad. I heard him say that he had heard the sheep and the birds talking about it amongst themselves.

HUGHES. Well, why shouldn't he? What about that lamb that spoke and prophesied——

ELVIN. Just a minute. You didn't hear it, did you?

HUGHES. No, I didn't, but lots of people did.

ELVIN. It's a funny thing, but I'm never there when these things happen. When I'm about, the only talking that lambs and sheep do is just *Baa*. (*He moves* R.)

HUGHES. Because you can't be there doesn't prove——

ELVIN (*turning to face* HUGHES *as he goes*). And that's what I say to you.

HUGHES. What?

ELVIN. Baa!

(*He goes out* R., *above the rock.*)

WICK (*rises, looks about, then crouches between* SHAW *and* HUGHES). Which way will we go from here?
SHAW. Down through Samaria and Judea. We'll have to have an Israelite guide.
WICK. What's Samaria like?
SHAW. Nothing much now. They say it used to be very rich—plenty of everything—but that's before my time.
HUGHES. The first time I ever came this way, I was only a child, and just when we got to Samaria, the Assyrians burst everything wide open and then let hell loose. They were rounding up the Samarians and driving 'em off like cattle. Towns, burning—or stinking with corpses. Kids being dragged out of their mothers' arms to be thrown to Moloch. Yes, and some of the fathers were offering their kids to Moloch themselves—feeding the furnaces with 'em.
WICK (*cautiously, dropping his voice*). My uncle hates Moloch.
HUGHES (*alarmed*). You be careful what you're saying.
WICK. All right. I'm only telling you two.
SHAW. Yes, but he's right, though. Keep it to yourself.
WICK (*almost in a whisper*). The Egyptian doesn't believe in Moloch.
HUGHES. He's got plenty of gods and goddesses of his own. You'll see. Bulls and snakes and cats. There's one with the head of a bird——
SHAW. There's two or three. And there's one with the head of a crocodile—Sebek. And in one of their lakes there's a big crocodile that is fed every day by the priests with meat and the finest meal.
HUGHES. But you never know what you're seeing down there in Egypt, there's so much sorcery. In all the towns there are hundreds of sorcerers and soothsayers, and they come up and stare at you—and begin telling your past and your future. There was an old blind sorcerer with a basket full of live snakes who came up to me once at Sais——

(*He breaks off abruptly because at this moment* DONNINGTON, *as the Egyptian, enters from* R. WICK *rises and faces* DONNINGTON. SHAW *rises and stands beside the box.*)

DONNINGTON (*who speaks with calm authority*). Has the guide arrived? (*He moves halfway up the ramp.*)
HUGHES (*rises*). No, not yet. Is he coming here?
DONNINGTON. That is what was arranged.
SHAW. Who is he?
DONNINGTON. I don't know. (*Moving down to stage level* R.C.) Probably some Israelite shepherd, who knows all the

mountain passes. If he does not come soon, we must go forward without him.

SHAW. Why? You said last night there was no hurry.

DONNINGTON. Now I know more than I knew last night. I know we cannot afford to linger here.

SHAW. The soldiers have told you something?

DONNINGTON (*calmly*). Yes, the soldiers have told me something.

(WICK *moves down from the rostrum and takes up a position down stage* L. *of* SHAW.)

HUGHES (*after a pause, uneasily*). Well—what did they tell you?

DONNINGTON. This morning, some of their horsemen, who were scouting in the north-east, came riding back at full speed to report that they had seen a vast moving cloud of dust, as if the very hills were shaking themselves—

HUGHES (*alarmed*). The Assyrians.

DONNINGTON. Yes, a large Assyrian army. (*Moving to* C.) It should pass well to the north of us, moving towards Phœnicia. But some of their horsemen might discover us here——

(HUGHES *moves down the ramp to stage level* R.)

SHAW. That's why the soldiers are getting ready to go.

DONNINGTON. Yes. Otherwise, their line of retreat may soon be cut off. They will be gone within an hour. And we should be going too, soon, for although the Assyrians may be old friends of yours, they are not friends of mine—or of Egypt.

SHAW. Don't worry. We don't like 'em any more than you do. But we've only these bits of things to pack up and then we can go, and once we're on the move south, they're not likely to find us.

(SHAW *and* WICK *pack up the bundles.*)

DONNINGTON. Very well. We will wait a little longer for the guide. It may save time in the end, for we could easily miss him, I imagine, once we have moved off, for he may be coming to us another way. (*Moving up on to the main centre of rock, he gazes over the desert.*)

HUGHES. Yes, we had better wait. (*He moves up the ramp on to the rostrum* R. *of* DONNINGTON. *More humbly.*) Tell me, Master, for you are a learned scribe, what is the little god there? (*He points to the idol.*)

DONNINGTON (*glancing at it and shrugging*). A piece of rough carved stone, my friend. No god at all. A barbarian image. But I think I have seen you praying to it once or twice.

HUGHES. Well, what if you have? I don't like taking any chances, these days. He—it—might have power in these parts.

DONNINGTON. Pray to it if it pleases you. But don't ask me to join you. (*Sitting on the* R. *corner of the rostrum.*)
WICK (*timidly*). Haven't you such gods and images in Egypt, sir?
DONNINGTON (*smiling*). We have everything in Egypt. We have learning and knowledge, and we have ignorance.
(HUGHES *sits above and to* R. *of* DONNINGTON.)
We have great families who have given us governors and high priests and exquisite princesses from time immemorial. We have scribes and architects and craftsmen. We have humble peasants. We have slaves of every colour—and black savages from the mountains and forests beyond Ethiopia. We have a civilization that has endured for thousands of years, and that will endure for ever.
WICK. Greater than Assyria? (*Sitting on the ledge of the rostrum, below and* L. *of* DONNINGTON.)
DONNINGTON (*contemptuously*). You talk like a child. Yesterday, Assyria did not exist, and to-morrow it will not exist. It is a thing of to-day. Before Assyria was heard of, Babylon was great, and may be great again—for Babylon was a civilization of a kind and not a mere plundering military machine—but long before Babylon was built, Egypt was a whole world in itself, and had raised the great pyramids and carved the everlasting Sphinx. I had an old master who worshipped Thoth the moon-god, and by fasting could put himself into a trance, free himself from time, and so gaze into the far future. He told me something of these visions—only a little, for I was very young and not fit for such knowledge—and he said he had seen strange and incomprehensible things—horseless chariots that went as fast as the wind—men inside great metal birds—men making wars—for always there were wars, as to-day—with thunder and lightning and vast invisible javelins—but even so, Egypt was still there—and the great pyramids still cast their mighty shadows—and the noble Sphinx still gazed across the desert. That—is Egypt.

(*There is a moment's silence. Then* ELVIN *comes bustling in* R., *looking excited and stands on the ramp facing* DONNINGTON.)

ELVIN. Have you told them?
DONNINGTON. No, I was waiting for you to join us.
ELVIN (*who cannot keep it to himself*). One of us has got to go with 'em.
(WICK *rises and moves* L.)
HUGHES (*rising*). With the soldiers?
ELVIN. Yes, and they're packing up now. (*He moves down to stage level, facing* SHAW.)

SHAW. Why should one of us go with 'em ? They know the way they want to go better than any of us would.
ELVIN. Don't ask me, ask him.
(*They look uneasily at* DONNINGTON, *who adopts a smooth but rather evasive manner. He rises and comes to* C.)
DONNINGTON. I was about to tell you. But I cannot give you the reason. I can only tell you that their captain insisted. Perhaps he is not sure of the roads and needs a guide. He wanted to take you all, but I pointed out that I had his commander's promise that this caravan should go safely south, and he knew that I had a mission to fulfil in Jerusalem—some gifts for King Hezekiah—before going on to Egypt. All that was settled with the Arameans, who are now the allies of Egyp So the captain agreed only to take one of you. But one of you will have to go with him, he declared, or he would take you all. (*He moves away, looking at* WICK.)
HUGHES (*uneasily*). Which one ?
DONNINGTON. He did not care which one went. And neither do I, for I shall be certain of having at least two experienced men left with me.
SHAW. You'd be certain of three—if he (*pointing to* WICK) went back with the soldiers.
WICK (*in alarm*). I don't want to go with them. Why should I ? Just because I'm the youngest. That's not fair. You don't know what's going to happen to those chaps or what they're up to. They always seemed to me a horrible tough gang. I'm not going back with them.
SHAW. And if you won't, why should one of us ?
ELVIN (*crossing to* DONNINGTON). Well, we'll have to draw lots, that's all.
HUGHES (*moving down to* R. *of* ELVIN). Now wait a minute, every time I've ever drawn lots with you, I've been unlucky.
SHAW. And so have I.
ELVIN. Listen to 'em. I can't help it if I'm lucky, can I ? You ought to have bought one of them lucky charms, same as I did, that time in Tyre. Best lucky charm I ever had, and I've still got it. So look out.
SHAW (*to* DONNINGTON). You shall arrange the drawing of the lots.
DONNINGTON. Very well.
ELVIN. Four pieces of stick will do, one shorter than the other three. I'll get 'em for you. (*He moves up as if to exit* R.)
HUGHES (*alarmed*). Oh—no, you won't. (*He stops* ELVIN.)
DONNINGTON. It will not be necessary. I have some. I will get them.
(*He goes out* R., *below the rock. The others glance at each other uneasily.* WICK *sits on a bundle* L. ELVIN *sits on the lower*

ledge, R.C. *He takes out a charm attached to a cord or chain round his neck, holds it up and strokes and kisses it.* SHAW *watches stolidly at* L.C. WICK, *after glancing at the others, then sits still and his mouth moves, as if he were silently praying. Meanwhile,* HUGHES *has been attracted to the idol again, has gone nearer to it, and finally drops down on his knees below it, bowing and supplicating.* JOSEPH *enters from up* L. *and stands looking at* HUGHES.)

JOSEPH. Why do you bow down to wood and stone?

(*All four look round, startled.* HUGHES *scrambles to his feet.* WICK *rises and goes down stage* L.)

HUGHES. What's that to do with you?
JOSEPH. I hate to see a man wasting his time and energy. What's the use of asking that lump of stone for anything? It can't hear. It can't see. It doesn't know you're there.
SHAW. Are you an Israelite?
JOSEPH. Of the tribe of Judah.
ELVIN. You must be the guide we've been waiting for.
JOSEPH (*moving down* C. *to the edge of the rostrum*). Not unless you have with you a certain Egyptian scribe.
ELVIN. He's back there. Be here in a minute. We four have to draw lots, because one of us must go off with the Aramean soldiers, damn their eyes!

(HUGHES *moves down* L.C., *near* SHAW.)

JOSEPH. Why are they in such a hurry to go, these Arameans?
ELVIN. There's a big Assyrian army coming from the northeast. If you know the Assyrians——
JOSEPH. I do. It's as if lions came swarming as thick as locusts, except that they are crueller than lions. (*He looks across* R.) But this must be the Egyptian.

(*Enter* DONNINGTON R. *He is carrying four short ivory sticks. He acknowledges the salutation of* JOSEPH *with gracious politeness.*)

DONNINGTON (*stands on top of the ramp at* R.C.). You are the guide sent by Shemer to lead us down to Jerusalem?
JOSEPH. I am.
DONNINGTON. You know the passes between Samaria into Judea?
JOSEPH. Yes. I am of Judah myself, but I know also all the country of Ephraim, all the lost kingdom of the ten northern tribes.
HUGHES. I was saying—earlier on—how I went through there—as a child—when the Assyrians put paid to that lot——

JOSEPH (*sternly, turning to* HUGHES). The word of the prophet was fulfilled.

DONNINGTON. What prophet was that ? You Israelites have so many prophets.

JOSEPH (*turning to* DONNINGTON). The prophet Amos, who was, as I am, a simple herdman, before Jehovah spoke in his voice. (*Looking around at them.*) He came suddenly to the great festival at Bethel, where the nobles and the rich men and their painted women and the false priests were drinking wine and sacrificing to the Bull and dancing before the image of Ashtoreth ; and he cried to them :

> " The Lord will roar from Zion,
> And utter his voice from Jerusalem ;
> And the habitations of the shepherds shall mourn ;
> And the top of Carmel shall wither."

And again he cried to them :

> " Hear this word, ye kine of Bashan,
> That are in the mountains of Samaria,
> Which oppress the poor, which crush the needy,
> Which say to their masters, ' Bring and let us drink,'
> The Lord God hath sworn by his holiness,
> That, lo, the days shall come upon you,
> That he will take you away with hooks,
> And your posterity with fishhooks."

WICK (*astonished and impressed, moving to* JOSEPH *at* C.). Who is this Lord God ?

JOSEPH (*turning to* WICK). I will answer you in the words of that same prophet Amos :

> " . . . Ye who turn judgment to wormwood,
> And leave off righteousness in the earth,
> Seek him that maketh the seven stars and Orion,
> And turneth the shadow of death into the morning
> And maketh the day dark with night :
> That calleth for the waters of the sea
> And poureth them out upon the face of the earth ;
> The Lord is his name."

(*He stands silent for a moment, facing front, while the others stare at him wonderingly, then he turns away and sits down.*)

DONNINGTON (*after a pause, holding up the sticks and coming to below the ledge of rock* R.C.). Here are the four sticks. One is shorter than the other three. He who draws the short stick must go with the soldiers. You are agreed ?

ELVIN. All right to me.

SHAW. And me. I'll take my chance.

HUGHES (*hesitating*). So will I—so long as there's no trickery.

DONNINGTON (*to* WICK). And you?
WICK (*doubting, fearful*). Yes—I suppose so—but——
ELVIN. But what?
WICK (*ashamed*). I am afraid. I don't want to go with them.
JOSEPH (*turning to look at them*). If this youth is afraid—and I can see he is—why don't you three, who are older, draw lots and so leave him with us?
DONNINGTON (*smoothly*). No, that wouldn't do. He must take his chance with the others. Now see—(*he shows them the ends of the four sticks, hiding their length*) you have only to take one of these——
HUGHES (*worried*). No Egyptian conjuring and trickery, mind.
SHAW. Let the Israelite hold the sticks, then.
JOSEPH. No. (*He rises.*) I'll have nothing to do with this. One of the older men should go.
ELVIN. You mind your own business.
JOSEPH (*sternly*). There is something evil here.
DONNINGTON. We are merely settling something among ourselves that does not concern you, my friend. It was already arranged before you arrived. You were not sent to us to be our guide on all matters, but only to lead us through your barbaric mountain passes. Keep your mind on your own affairs. Work out the quickest route from here as far as Jerusalem.
JOSEPH. I smell death. (*He climbs the ledge of rock to the back of the rostrum and stands facing up stage.*)
ELVIN. Oh—give it a rest—you're worse than he is. (*Indicating* HUGHES.)
DONNINGTON. We waste time. Now choose. (*He holds out the sticks as before.*)
ELVIN. All right. Now's your chance again, my old lucky charm. (*He touches his charm, and then goes forward and takes a stick.*)
SHAW (*going forward*). Here, let's have a look. (*He goes forward, and after staring hard at the sticks, he chooses one.*)
HUGHES (*in sudden alarm*). Only two left!
DONNINGTON (*amused*). Yes, but they may be two long ones. The chance is the same.
HUGHES (*looking at the sticks*). Wait a minute now! That one.

(*He takes one.* DONNINGTON *now holds up the last one to* WICK, *who comes forward shakily and takes it. It is the short one, though this is not obvious at first.*)

DONNINGTON. Now show me.

(*They show him the sticks in their hands. He points to* WICK, *who gives a smothered cry.* JOSEPH *turns and looks down at the group.*)

Fortune was against you.

(WICK *moves slowly to the bundle down* L., *and sits.*)

ELVIN. Sorry about that, boy. Never mind. Won't be too bad.

HUGHES. No, of course not. For a youngster like yourself, there's nothing like going off with a troop of soldiers.

WICK (*slowly, carefully*). You needn't say any more. I'm not afraid now. Somehow, it's different now.

ELVIN. That's right. Took it too seriously, before.

WICK. No. It is now that I know how serious it is. But I'm not afraid.

(*He looks across at* JOSEPH, *who is now regarding him gravely and, rising, moves up* R.C., *below the idol.*)

You were right.

DONNINGTON (*moving down* R.). I am sorry, but you will have to hurry. Get your things.

ELVIN. Oh—we'll get his things. And see him off.

SHAW. Come on, boy.

(ELVIN *takes up one of the bundles and* SHAW *takes another, and with* HUGHES *they exit up* R. *Meanwhile,* JOSEPH *has moved down towards* WICK. *They regard each other gravely.*)

JOSEPH. There is something you wish me to do—or to say— —what is it?

WICK (*hesitatingly*). This Jehovah—this Lord God—of yours

JOSEPH. Yes?

WICK. Is he a sun god?

JOSEPH (*down to* C.). He is the maker of suns. And moons and stars.

WICK. What is his image like?

JOSEPH. He has no image. We of the tribe of Judah who keep the word do not worship images. It was the worship of images that brought ruin upon the ten tribes.

DONNINGTON (*coming to* R.C.). There's no time now for Hebrew history. This youth must go.

WICK (*rather desperately*). Where is he—this Lord God?

JOSEPH. He is on high.

WICK (*distressed, moving a little down stage*). No—I do not understand. And I must go. (*He turns to face* JOSEPH.) But there was something you said about the seven stars and Orion. Say it again to me before I go, so that I may remember it.

JOSEPH (*slowly*). "Seek him that maketh the seven stars and Orion,

And turneth the shadow of death into the morning."

DONNINGTON (*sharply*). You must go now.

WICK (*slowly*). And turneth the shadow of death into the morning.

(*He smiles, nods gratefully to* JOSEPH, *and then exits slowly up* R. JOSEPH *stares after him sombrely.* DONNINGTON, *relieved, sits down on the rock* R.C. *and smiles.*)

DONNINGTON (*after a pause*). We must be going soon. As soon as the soldiers have moved off, I will tell the men to pack up these things—for the animals are already loaded—and then we can go. Take us by the shortest route to Samaria, and then by the quickest roads through that country into Judah.

JOSEPH (*abstractedly*). Yes. (*Moving away a little* L.C.).

DONNINGTON. You Israelites of the old faith have some curious and fanatical notions. (*He rises.*) For instance, didn't I hear you telling that youth that it was the worship of images that brought ruin upon your ten Northern tribes? (*He moves to the edge of the rostrum, at* C.)

JOSEPH. That is what I said. It is what our prophets have told us. There is in Jerusalem now a great prophet—Isaiah——

DONNINGTON. Yes, I have heard of Isaiah.

JOSEPH (*turning to face* DONNINGTON). He is old now, but he goes barefoot and almost naked, looking like a captive slave, to warn the people of Judah——

DONNINGTON. Yes, I have heard. To warn them against rebellion against Assyria, to denounce the new Egyptian alliance. And now you are going to tell me you have heard this same Isaiah declare that it was the worship of images—as you call it—that brought ruin to the ten tribes and the Northern kingdom.

JOSEPH (*moving* L. *to the hump by the idol and sitting*). Yes, I have heard him tell the people that. He is a great preacher.

DONNINGTON. But don't you see the absurdity of these ideas? The Northern kingdom fell simply because it couldn't stand up against the powerful Assyrian army. Purely a military problem. Nothing to do with the worship of images at all.

JOSEPH. You did not listen to the words of the prophet Amos that I recited. He said to the greedy nobles and the false priests: " Ye who turn judgment to wormwood, and leave off righteousness in the earth——"

DONNINGTON. Very striking, no doubt. You Israelites are excellent poets. But not so effective as the striking power of the Assyrian heavy and light cavalry and their first-class archery.

JOSEPH. You are like so many. You have knowledge but no wisdom. You have clear sight but no insight. The herdman Amos could see further than you and all the priests and scribes in Egypt.

DONNINGTON (*smiling*). Now you are behaving like a barbarian. You cannot reply to my argument and so you become abusive. Turning judgment to wormwood, leaving off righteousness, worshipping images—what have they to do with the facts of the military problem?

JOSEPH (*with emphasis*). Because a kingdom in which judgment has turned to wormwood and there is no righteousness is like a fruit that has gone rotten, and will crumble at a touch. Because when the Israelite has forsaken the pure worship of the Lord God, when he bows down to images and throws his children into the furnaces of Moloch and sends his daughters to prostitute themselves for Ashtoreth, then he has allowed himself to be conquered from within before the invader has shot the first arrow. The rich will not fight because they are lost in greed, drunkenness, lechery and sloth; and the poor will not fight because they have been oppressed and crushed, and they feel that the new masters cannot be any worse than the old. It is Baal and Moloch and Ashtoreth, the false gods and goddesses of cruelty and filth, that conquer the world; and the archers and chariots of Assyria only occupy the kingdoms already fallen and lost.

DONNINGTON. These are not the gods of Egypt, nor is Egypt among such kingdoms.

JOSEPH. The turn of Egypt will surely come. I have heard Isaiah cry out against the trust in Egypt that has taken the place of the trust in the Lord. " Woe to them," he cried, " that walk to go down into Egypt and have not asked at the mouth of the Lord God; to strengthen themselves in the strength of Pharaoh, and to trust in the shadow of Egypt. Therefore shall the strength of Pharaoh be your shame, and the trust in the shadow of Egypt your confusion."

DONNINGTON. What would your prophet have his king and people do? Obey the Assyrians?

JOSEPH. No, obey the Lord God. " In returning and rest shall ye be saved," he told them. " In quietness and in confidence shall be your strength : and ye would not."

DONNINGTON. Egypt is already very old, and time cannot touch her. We have prophets too—though they speak and act very differently from these strange wild men of yours—and sometimes they peer through the mists of the centuries—far into the future—but always they see Egypt, the great pyramids and the ever-enduring Sphinx.

JOSEPH. What they see is nothing but an enduring sepulchre. The stones will be there but the greatness and quickness of life will have gone. The glory of Egypt is fading now. The sun is setting across the Nile, the shadows gather, and the long night is coming.

DONNINGTON (*indifferently*). It may be so. But it does not

matter. Our wisest men, who know the mysteries of Osiris and Isis, and have travelled in spirit with Anubis across the kingdoms of the dead, tell us that life is but a dream.

JOSEPH. That is idle talk. If it is a dream, it is a dream in which you bleed, and vomit in your sickness, and hear your children cry out in terror before they are tossed on to the spears of the invader. It is a dream in which Egypt gives place to Babylon and Babylon to Assyria, and Assyria—it may be—to the Medes and the men of the northern mountains—and after them—it may be to the brazen men—as the prophet said——

DONNINGTON (*interested*). What prophet is this—Isaiah again——?

JOSEPH. No, his disciple Micah, who had many visions on the mountain near my home—and would come down to tell us what he had seen. There were brazen men who came like a thunderbolt and conquered the world again—and after them many others—from the East—from the West—men of bronze— men of iron—men with ships—men with strange beasts——

DONNINGTON (*rather eagerly*). And men who fought with thunder and lightning and invisible javelins—and men who came inside great metal birds——

JOSEPH. You have heard him?

DONNINGTON. No. My old master—a priest of Thoth— once told me these things.

JOSEPH. Micah had many such visions on the mountain. Great vessels on the sea larger than the Ark built by Noah and his sons—and cities far greater than Jerusalem or Nineveh, Babylon or Memphis—with towers that reached to the sky—as high as the tower of Babel—and vast magical contrivances that would do with ease in a day the labour of ten thousand men. And yet, said Micah, these visions too were filled with fire and blood, anger and suffering, and there was still desolation in men's hearts because they worshipped false gods (*he rises*)—yes, and judgment was still turned to wormword, and men left off righteousness. As it is now, so it will be then. Did I not hear the prophet cry (*he moves to the centre of the rostrum*):

"They built up Zion with blood,
And Jerusalem with iniquity.
The heads thereof judge for reward,
And the priests thereof teach for hire,
And the prophets thereof divine for money:
Yet will they lean upon the Lord, and say,
 'Is not the Lord among us?
 None evil can come upon us.'
Therefore shall Zion for your sake be ploughed as a field,
And Jerusalem shall become heaps,
And the mountain of the house of the Lord as the high places of the forest."

DONNINGTON (*after a pause, sitting on the ledge of rocks*). I tell you, Israelite, that to me—an Egyptian and a scribe—who have seen many countries and peoples and belong to the oldest of them, whose ancestors were living in courts and temples when yours lived savagely in the desert with their animals, these are only the wild visions and crazed sayings of some barbarian half-mad with fasting and loneliness—and yet, I will confess, they move me quite strangely. It may be only the chanting fury and fire of your voice. We sing very different songs to our little harps in Egypt.

JOSEPH (*gruffly*). We have our songs. But these are the inspired words of the prophets through whom our Lord God speaks. Enough!

(*He turns aside.* JOSEPH *moves away* L.C., *on to the ramp.*)

DONNINGTON (*after a pause*). What is the matter? Have I offended you?

JOSEPH. No.

DONNINGTON. What is it, then?

JOSEPH. I wish to be gone from this place.

DONNINGTON (*rising, moving to* C.). So do I. I am only waiting for the three men to return.

JOSEPH. There is terror in the air, and I smell death.

DONNINGTON. You could find terror in the air, and could smell death, everywhere these days. (*Moving down* L.) For life now is like a dark violent dream, whereas in the days of my ancestors it was like a clear tranquil dream, when a man's three score years passed like the shadow of a bird across a sunlit garden. (*He turns.*) Then a man might labour lightly all his life at one pleasant task—carving the head of a god, painting the triumphs of a Pharaoh, filling the pools and tending the flower-beds outside a temple—and watch his children, and his children's children, grow—and sleep in peace. The golden age has gone, and we have entered the age of iron.

JOSEPH. You do not need to teach a Hebrew that.

DONNINGTON (*returning slowly to* C.). Yet we Egyptians once taught you many things, and there are still some things you might learn.

JOSEPH (*fiercely, facing* DONNINGTON). There is nothing—— (*He breaks off, turning away sharply.*)

DONNINGTON (*after a pause*). Well?

JOSEPH. No. I spoke then out of pride. It is our greatest fault—this fierce and challenging pride. So I stopped my mouth. (*He comes down* L.C.)

DONNINGTON (*sitting on the* R. *downstage corner of the rostrum*). You should rest before the journey.

JOSEPH. I am uneasy.

DONNINGTON. Why?

JOSEPH (*crosses* L. *to the boxes and turns*). What will become of the youth who left us ?
DONNINGTON (*rather evasively*). I don't know. The captain of the soldiers demanded that one of the men should go with them, and I had no choice but to agree.
JOSEPH (*taking a few paces towards* C.). And that is all you know ?
DONNINGTON. That is all.
JOSEPH. I saw the shadow of death in the face of that youth.

(*Suddenly going closer and staring into* DONNINGTON'S *face*.)

And you are lying.
DONNINGTON (*rising*). What ? (*He steps towards* JOSEPH.)
JOSEPH (*fiercely*). You are lying.

(*He looks as if he is about to strike* DONNINGTON, *but he checks himself. The two men stare at each other.*)

DONNINGTON (*slowly*). Your countryman, Shemer, swore to me by his faith in your God that he would send me a guide who would see me safely to Jerusalem—on my way to Memphis. Have you too sworn to him to do this ?
JOSEPH (*regretfully*). He has my word.
DONNINGTON (*smiling*). Then you must keep it.
JOSEPH. I shall keep it. (*He moves down a pace* L.C.)
DONNINGTON. But you sound regretful.
JOSEPH. I am. If I were free to do what I please, I would go back the way I came—alone. (*He turns to face* DONNINGTON.) There is something here I do not like, and already you have lied to me.

(DONNINGTON *steps back a pace to the edge of the rocks* C.)

I saw the shadow of death in that boy's face.

(HUGHES *enters* R., *panting, as if he had been running, and very excited.*)

HUGHES (*at* R.C., *pointing back*). Master—master—they have seized the youth and bound him before their altar of the Baal —we could—do nothing——
DONNINGTON. And I can do nothing.
JOSEPH (*fiercely, shouting*). I will curse their foul image—— (*He runs towards the ramp*, R.C.)
DONNINGTON. Stop him !

(HUGHES *prevents* JOSEPH *from going out*. SHAW *and* ELVIN *now arrive* R., *and assist* HUGHES.)

(*To* SHAW *and* ELVIN). Stop this Israelite—or they'll kill him too—and we'll have no guide.

(*They struggle for a moment, preventing* JOSEPH *from going out* R. *Then a distant shout—as if made simultaneously by a large body of men—is heard. The struggle ceases at once, and they all stare off* R. JOSEPH *backs slowly to down* C.)

SHAW (*slowly*). They shout because the god has accepted the sacrifice. (*He turns down* R.)

ELVIN. We saw them bind him to the altar. They were all waiting for him—cruel swine, they're as bad as the Assyrians.

HUGHES. Now they're already beginning to march away.

ELVIN. Poor little devil—no Nineveh or Memphis or anything else for him!

(JOSEPH *turns away, mounts the rostrum slowly, sick at heart, moving to the* L.C. *end.*)

DONNINGTON (*moving down C., and turning to face the men* R.). We must go now—and quickly. (*Then turning to* JOSEPH.) Remember, your word is pledged.

JOSEPH (*bitterly, his back to* DONNINGTON). I have not forgotten.

DONNINGTON. I could do nothing. (*To* L.C., *below and behind* JOSEPH.) The captain insisted that they must have the youth for a sacrifice, and was sending men to fetch him—but I thought it would be better for the youth if I pretended he was merely going with them—and the drawing of the lots was a mere trick——

JOSEPH (*turning to face* DONNINGTON). You could have given him the swiftest animal and told him to escape——

DONNINGTON. Then we should all have been killed. (*Turning to the three men.*) Pack up these things. We must go at once. Hurry, hurry!

(*He moves to* R., *as* WICK, SHAW *and* ELVIN *cross down stage* L. *to the boxes*).

JOSEPH (*moving back to the centre of the rostrum*). I was wrong to say that we must leave this place. Why should we make haste? We go from one place of evil only to another, and our iniquity goes with us.

(*They stop and stare at him in bewilderment. He faces the front.*)

"Then said I, Lord, how long? And he answered, Until the cities be wasted without inhabitant, and the houses without man, and the land be utterly desolate . . ." (*He pauses for a moment, then cries with a kind of fierce exultation, dominating the scene.*) "And what will ye do in the day of visitation, and in the desolation which shall come from far? To whom will we flee for help? And where will ye leave your glory?"

As he stands there, and they stare at him—
The CURTAIN *falls.*

ACT II

The SCENE *is now as it was in Act I. But it is full morning.*
SHAW *and* HUGHES *are sitting at each side of a ground sheet spread on the stage* C. SHAW *is on the* L. *of* HUGHES. *They are busy cleaning a machine gun. They are also sharing one cigarette, and arguing loudly about football. The others cannot be seen.*

HUGHES (*who has the cigarette, contemptuously*). Huddersfield!

SHAW (*aggressively*). Yes, 'Uddersfield. 'Ere, come on.

(*He reaches for the cigarette, then takes a deep drag at it while* HUGHES *watches him anxiously.*)

HUGHES. Huddersfield! Nothing to me, nothing at all! (*He takes the cigarette.*)

SHAW. Ah dare say. But they played better football nor Cardiff City ever did. 'Ere, an' go easy wi' that fag. It's like sharin' a fag with a suction pump.

HUGHES. Cardiff City. I care nothing at all about Cardiff City. Why—we don't think of Cardiff as a Welsh town at all. Swansea—Port Talbot—of course—very different—but Cardiff —no, we never think of it as a proper Welsh town. English— really.

SHAW. English! Course it's not English. Nay, Ah knaw better nor that. Yer can't get aht of it that way.

HUGHES (*annoyed, loudly*). Get out of it! Let me tell you, I'm not trying to get out of anything. You won't stick to the point, man, that's your trouble, won't stick to the point.

SHAW (*equally annoyed*). Nah nobody can say Ah don't stick to t' point. You started by sayin' that under this Beveridge Report every chap gets at least two pahnd ten a week——

HUGHES (*excitedly*). And then you talk about football and say what about Cardiff City—and I tell you I care nothing about Cardiff City——

SHAW (*very loudly*). Yer went on abaht 'Uddersfield, didn't yer?

HUGHES (*very loudly*). I only mentioned Huddersfield because you were beginning to insult Wales——

(ELVIN *now comes out of the tent, where he has been looking after* WICK. *His ferocious expression stops both men as he comes across to* L.C.)

ELVIN (*softly but very fiercely*). Turn it up—for Gawd's sake— turn it up. 'Ere's this poor little bleeder—won't tike nothin'— don't know nobody—ready to 'and his bleedin' check in—an' all you two muckers can do is to argue the toss top o' yer voices. Get the Sergeant—pronto.

HUGHES (*hastily*). I'll tell him.

(*He hurries off* R., *below the tank, while* SHAW *goes with* ELVIN *back to the tent and looks in.*)

SHAW (*dubiously*). 'Ow are yer, Georgie?

ELVIN (*quietly but urgently*). No use asking 'im. I tried that. But 'e don't know nobody—see? Talks to 'is mum an' dad an' 'is brother sometimes—see? But the pore little bleeder don't know none of us—'e don't know 'e's 'ere.

SHAW. Delirious—that's what 'e is.

ELVIN. I know, I know. I seen blokes like that when you was just learnin' to walk. When they're bad—yer see, Yorkie —they don't know where they are or what's 'appened to 'em— that's nature, see?

SHAW. Better like that, in't it?

ELVIN. Course it is. Bit o' kindness on Nature's part, that is, chummie. I've seen blokes wiv legs an' arms off—nuthink of 'em left, yer might say—finished an' for it, of course—but they didn't know nuthink jus' felt a bit cold, that's all.

SHAW (*disgusted*). Arms an' legs off. Ah think we're all wrong in our 'eads. (*He moves to down* C.)

(SERGEANT JOSEPH *hurries in from* R., *below the tank, followed by* DONNINGTON.)

JOSEPH. He's worse, is he? (*Joining* ELVIN *at up* L.C., *with* DONNINGTON.)

ELVIN. Looks like it ter me, Sergeant. I can't do nuthink more for 'im. An' I thought I better go for some more water. (*He moves to down* C., *and turns. Wistfully :*) Yer a clever bloke, Sergeant. Can't yer think o' something we could do for 'im?

(SHAW *moves to his original position up* C., *sits and assembles the Bren.*)

JOSEPH (*moving* L., *and looking into the tent*). I'm afraid not, Knocker. I've done all I can think of. If he was in hospital they'd probably give him a blood transfusion.

ELVIN (*seriously*). 'E can 'ave a pint o' mine at any time.

JOSEPH. I know. But we couldn't work it. Don't even know if it would be the right thing to do. Well, I'll look after him now.

ELVIN. I'll go an' brew some char.

(*He goes out* R. *in front of the tank.*)

JOSEPH. Shaw, when you've finished cleaning that gun, **go** and join Hughes in the Tank and see if you can do anything with the wireless.

SHAW. Right-o, Sergeant.

(JOSEPH *goes into the tent.* DONNINGTON *moves to* R. *of* C., *and sits down with* SHAW.)

DONNINGTON (*as he sits*). I'll give you a hand with this.

SHAW. Can't yer get owt o' that wireless?

DONNINGTON. Not a thing.

SHAW. It's all right, isn't it?

DONNINGTON. Yes, *it's* all right. What's wrong is us. We're clean out of touch. We're lost.

SHAW. Well, if it depends on yon tank to get us out of it, we'll stay lost. It'll tak' lads in workshops a week or two to get 'er goin' again.

DONNINGTON (*gloomily*). If you ask me, by this time there's a few hundred miles of desert between us and the rest of the division. We don't know where they are, and they don't know where we are.

SHAW. That's abaht it, Corporal. But 'appen they'll send a recce plane.

DONNINGTON (*mocking him*). 'Appen they will an' all. But don't forget, one plane has spotted us already. That one of theirs, last night.

SHAW. Ay, Ah wor forgettin' that. Well, what we goin' ter do?

DONNINGTON. Well, we're not going to start walking it.

SHAW. No fear. Besides, if we did, where'd we go?

DONNINGTON. You've said it. Where would we go? So we'll just have to stop here until somebody finds us.

SHAW. They'd better be sharp. We 'aven't much water in tank, an' that stuff along there's fairly crawlin'—an' there's none so much o' that. Ah went along there this mornin' wi' Knocker. An' then what about rations? Ah feels 'ungry now.

DONNINGTON. Then we'd better change the subject. What about Ossett? And those two girls you can't make up your mind about—what are their names?

SHAW. Nellie and Olive.

DONNINGTON (*reflectively*). I feel like Olive to-day. How about you?

SHAW. Either'd do me, though Ah'd rather 'ave a good meat tea.

(DONNINGTON *rises and crosses to the tank.*)

Aaa!—when Ah think what Ah used to grumble at when Ah wor at 'ome, nay, Ah could kick meself, Ah could. Ah didn't know Ah wor born.

DONNINGTON (*sitting* R., *left of the tank*). I dreamt last night

I was sitting down to roast duck and green peas with a beautiful blonde called Paula. And the wine waiter at the Savoy Grill—who for some reason or other looked and talked just like my Uncle Archie—was opening some champagne. But what the hell! I wasn't happy when I had all that, and now I'm miserable because I haven't it. What's the matter with us, Shaw?

SHAW. Ah don't know about you. But Ah can tell yer what's matter wi' me. Ah'm stuck 'ere in t'bloody desert, an' Ah don't know 'ow Ah'm goin' ter get aht of it.

DONNINGTON (*rising*). We've always been stuck in a desert, if you ask me.

SHAW. Nay, Ah 'aven't. Ossett's no desert.

DONNINGTON (*moving to below the rocks* R.C.). I'll bet it would have looked like one to me. (*Quoting with rich but mocking emphasis.*) " The wilderness and the solitary place shall be glad for them ; and the desert shall rejoice, and blossom as the rose." What a hope! But what words, eh? I can feel 'em down my spine.

SHAW. Well, Ah can't. An' it's not words but a 'ell of a lot of water this desert 'ud 'ave before it starts blossoming as a rose.

DONNINGTON (*mockingly*). The Water of Life, Herbert, the Water of Life. (*He changes the subject abruptly.*) Well, in a way I hope they do find us. (*He comes down stage and crosses* L.C.)

SHAW. Yer mean—the Jerries?

DONNINGTON. Yes. Then either we can make a fight of it——or we can't. And either way, it would be better than rotting away here.

JOSEPH (*coming out of the tent*). Drop it, Phil. We're not rotting away yet.

DONNINGTON (*moving down* L.). Speak for yourself, Ben. I've been doing it quietly for years. (*Turning.*) How is he?

JOSEPH. He's a lot weaker. No pain. Seems quite comfortable, in fact. But I feel that's a bad sign.

DONNINGTON (*quietly*). Is he delirious?

JOSEPH. Yes, wandering a bit, poor kid.

(ELVIN *enters* R. *with two mugs of tea.*)

ELVIN (*crossing to* L.C.). Cuppa char any good to 'im, Sarge?

JOSEPH. 'Fraid not, Knocker.

ELVIN. You 'ave one, Sarge?

JOSEPH. No, thanks. Give it to the others. (*He enters the tent.*)

ELVIN (*approaching the other two*). Cuppa sergeant-major's, Corporal?

DONNINGTON. Not for me, thanks, Knocker. Believe it or not, I don't like sergeant-major's tea.

ELVIN (*incredulous*). Go orn!

DONNINGTON. Fact. I'm not a real soldier at all, I haven't

got the right ideas. (*He sits on a sandbag* L.) Shaw here'll drink it.

ELVIN (*handing* SHAW *one mug, and moves to* R. *of the ground sheet*). I'll bet 'e will. Knows what's good for 'im, ol' Yorky does, silly as 'e looks. (*He sits down and drinks.*)

SHAW. Ah'll drink 'alf and tak' rest to Hughes, eh?

(*He drinks.*)

ELVIN (*meditatively*). Yer can't believe it, can yer?

DONNINGTON. Believe what? that you're here?

ELVIN (*leaning on his left elbow, facing down* L.). The 'ole flamin' carry-on. I starts thinkin'—see?—while I'm brewin' that char. Yer know 'ow things comes into the ol' loaf. I starts thinkin' o' the time after the last war when five 'undred of us comes back from India—see? An' I'm goin' ter get my ticket. An' every bleedin' thing goes my way that time—see? I'm just Dick Bloody Whittington. If they'd made me Lord Mayor, I wouldn't ha' bin surprised—though I wouldn't ha' touched it, nacherally. But I'm comin' back to get my ticket, see? An' plenty o' back pay an' special allowances. All right. Well, me an' a bloke called Kelly starts workin' the mudhook on the ship, you know, the old Crown and Anchor, an' don't forget there's five 'undred of us—all paid up, see? Well, we can't go wrong. The bees an' 'oney rolls in, see? The only trouble is tryin' to stop the blokes you've taken it from all day takin' it back again when they think yer asleep at night, see? But me an' Kelly kips together an' we take it in turns to 'ave our bit of shut-eye. So we gets to Tilbury—an' my share's a 'undred an' twenty quid, see?

SHAW (*staggered*). 'Undred an' twenty quid—just out o' Crown an' Anchor!

ELVIN. As true as I'm 'ere. So I gets 'ome, drinks twelve bottles o' Guinness—an' sleeps for about two days, see? Then I gets up an' goes to a barber's for a shave—'cos now I'm in the money I don't do nothin' for myself, see? An' there's a bloke in there called Ernie Pott—Fat Pott, we all call 'im—an' e's a racin' bloke—used ter be a tic-tac man for a big bookie—an' I says "Wotcher, Fat Pott," an' 'e says, "Wotcher, me ol' cock sparrer"—an' I tells 'im I've just got me ticket an' back from India—an' what was the boys fancyin' for the Derby, see? So 'e tells me—Captain Cuttle–Steve Donoghue—an' 'e can get me tens. An' I can't go wrong, see? I puts seventy-five quid on Captain Cuttle—an' Steve brings 'im 'ome at ten ter one—an' I gets seven 'undred quid——

DONNINGTON. Why not seven hundred and fifty?

ELVIN. 'Cos I can't find one bookie—see? But I gets seven 'undred—an' I've still got a 'undred and fifty o' me own—so that's eight 'undred an' fifty quid—blimey, I felt like Solly Joel.

Blokes come miles just to 'ave a look at me. An' just 'cos I'd got plenty, I 'adn't to buy them their pig's ear—oh no—they'd buy the drinks for me—see ? Course they was after a big touch—nacherally—but I could ha' bin drunk for weeks on nuthin'—just 'cos I'd got plenty. An' there I was—got me ticket—paid off—eight 'undred an' fifty quid—an' couldn't go wrong. *An' look at me now.* I 'ad ter tell myself I'm still the same bloke. I begun to think it must 'ave 'appened to somebody else.

SHAW (*rising, taking the gun and the tea*). If Ah'd that much money, Ah'd 'ave bought a good milk round. (*He crosses* R.)

ELVIN (*contemptuously*). Milk round! Strewth, I wouldn't 'ave one given. Go on, tell it to Taffy in there. I bet 'e'd like a nice milk round too.

(DONNINGTON *rises to* L. *of the ground sheet and lies full length.* SHAW *goes out behind the tank.* ELVIN *makes a loud contemptuous noise.*)

If some of those blokes we got now 'ad bin soldering with the blokes I remember, they'd a bin torn to pieces. Like them young lads I met down at Cairo one time, who says, " We won a battle. We oughter go 'ome now." "Cripes," I says, " yer soldiers now, not stayin' in a ruddy 'oliday camp. They never used ter let us go 'ome till our mothers didn't know us."

JOSEPH (*looking out of the tent, quietly*). Phil. (*He withdraws.*)

(DONNINGTON *rises and goes into the tent.* ELVIN, *looking anxious, rises and goes uncertainly in that direction, finally glances in the tent. Then, scared by what he sees in there, he hurries across towards the ramp. In another moment, he returns with* HUGHES *and* SHAW, *and the three of them, deeply concerned, cross to the tent, and stand awkwardly looking down into it.* R. *of the group,* HUGHES' *lips are moving, and after a moment or two,* ELVIN, L. *of the group, notices this.*)

ELVIN (*seriously, in a whisper*). What yer mutterin' about ?
HUGHES (*seriously, but rather shamefacedly*). I was praying.
ELVIN (*same tone*). That's all right, china. Wish I could.

(*They are now quiet and motionless, and for a few moments there is complete silence. At the end of this time, the three men, looking deeply troubled, exchange meaning glances, and then* ELVIN *nods his head.* HUGHES *goes away and sits down,* R. *of the Bren gun, his back turned to the audience, holding his head in his hands. The other two, turned to stone, still stare dumbly at the tent. Then, slowly,* JOSEPH *and* DONNINGTON *come out of the tent.* JOSEPH *is carrying* WICK'S *identity disc, paybook, Bible, etc., and he slowly turns them over, as he moves to* C., *with* DONNINGTON.)

(*Very quietly.*) Better keep 'im in that blanket, 'adn't we, Sergeant ?

D

JOSEPH. Yes.
ELVIN (*hesitantly*). I'll just—sorta—see 'e's all right——

He goes into the tent. SHAW *moves slowly forward to the tent but does not go in.* JOSEPH *sits down on the ledge of rock below the idol.* DONNINGTON *moves* R. *restlessly, and then on to the ramp. He is obviously afraid of letting himself go.*)

DONNINGTON (*to* JOSEPH). Writing a report?
JOSEPH. Yes.
DONNINGTON (*at* C., *on the ramp, half sneering*). Think anybody on our side is ever going to see it?
JOSEPH (*looking up, steadily*). Yes. Whatever happens to us, they'll see it sooner or later. And anyhow, it's got to be written.
DONNINGTON. I wish I could take it as coolly as you can.
JOSEPH. Don't get me wrong, Phil. And this has got to be done—and I'd rather be doing something.

(ELVIN *now comes out of the tent, his face working and his voice unsteady.*)

ELVIN (*to* L.C.). Christ!—he only looks about ten now—like a school kid fast asleep. (*After a pause, as* SHAW *moves down* L. *a little.*) Are we leavin' 'im there, Sergeant?
JOSEPH (*looking up*). Yes, for the time being. But we can't leave him too long. If it doesn't look as if we can get away from here soon, then we'll have to bury him.
DONNINGTON (*with bitter emphasis*). Here lies the body of George Wick, private soldier, aged twenty, who left the best farm in Long Micklem, Gloucestershire, to be shot to bits in the Syrian Desert—and——
ELVIN (*going up to* DONNINGTON, L. *of the Bren gun, shouting furiously*). Yer don't 'ave to make a bleedin' mock o' the poor kid now, do yer? Stripes or no stripes, if I thought yer were makin' a mock of 'im (*threatening him with his fist*) I'd push this right down yer bleedin' throat—see?

(SHAW *turns to face* ELVIN *and* DONNINGTON. HUGHES *rises and faces them.*)

DONNINGTON (*angrily*). Why—you talkin' baboon—I was as fond of the kid as you were—and I'm not making a mock of him—as you call it. I'm only making a mock of the whole goddamned crazy set-up—and I'm doing it because if I don't try for a laugh, I'll either cry or go mad. What was he doing here, poor little devil? What are we all doing here? What's it all about, anyhow? We've had two of these wars, with a few assorted massacres and mass starvations in between, and I'll bet there are fat-bellied swine at home now making plans that'll land us into World War Number Three. If there has to be shooting, then let's go and shoot some of those jackasses and greedy-guts for a change——

JOSEPH (*getting up, sternly and walks over to* DONNINGTON). Corporal Donnington, if anything happens to me, you'll be in charge here.

DONNINGTON. So what?

(ELVIN *moves down* R.C.)

JOSEPH. That kind of talk isn't going to help the situation. What are men going to think if they hear an N.C.O. talking like that?

DONNINGTON (*tearing off the stripes from his left arm and throwing them down, angrily*). Take the stripes. I don't want 'em. Never did.

ELVIN (*turning to face* JOSEPH). Now listen, Sarge. 'E's upset, same as we all are. An' it's my fault, I thought 'e was making a mock o' poor young Georgie—see?

JOSEPH. All right, Elvin. I know all about it. Get back on your job. You two—(*to* HUGHES *and* SHAW)—as well. Come on now—get going.

(*The three men go out* R. *above the tank.* JOSEPH *watches them go, then turns to* DONNINGTON.)

Pick those stripes up, Corporal. You'll need 'em.

(DONNINGTON *picks them up, then looks at* JOSEPH *and sits on the ramp.*)

DONNINGTON. I'm sorry for that outburst, Ben.

JOSEPH. All right. Let's forget it. Knocker was quite right. That kid's death has knocked us all sideways—it's one thing seeing a few fellows killed in action, when you're too busy to take much notice, and it's quite another thing when it happens like this. So you had to let steam off.

(*He crosses* DONNINGTON *on to the ramp, looking up stage* R.)

DONNINGTON. Thanks, Ben. But there's more than that in it. I've been feeling it more and more for a long time now. A sort of angry despair. What the hell! Nobody learns anything. Nobody wants to. We're all wandering about in a colossal lunatic asylum. You heard what the ABCA chap at brigade headquarters said. Quite apart from the war casualties, which run into millions and millions on the Russian Front— over two million people executed in Poland, about three-quarters of a million in Yugoslavia, half a million deported to penal servitude in Czechoslovakia. Half Europe starving to death. Old men digging their graves. Schoolgirls shipped like cattle to brothels—

D*

(JOSEPH *descends from the ramp and moves to* L.C. *He turns on the word "* brothels.*"*)

JOSEPH (*sharply*). You needn't tell me these things. Haven't they been happening more to my people than to anybody else? (*Moving to* R. *of* C.)

DONNINGTON (*rather sharply*). All right, then, you're a Jew. (*He moves down stage to* JOSEPH'S L.) You know what's been happening to your people, even before this war started——

JOSEPH. Thousands of years before this war started. Two thousand five hundred years ago the Assyrians and then the Babylonians were driving my people into slavery—perhaps across this very ground we're standing on now. If that thing (*pointing to the top of the stone idol*) could speak, it could probably tell us a long, long tale of suffering—yes, of Jewish suffering.

DONNINGTON. I dare say it could. I know your history. But it's even worse now—don't forget that. The Nazis could teach the Assyrians and Babylonians and Egyptians a thing or two about slavery, torture and mass murder. Look what——

JOSEPH (*crosses* R. *up to* DONNINGTON—*sharply breaking in*). I say, you needn't tell me. I *know*. I don't only know it here—(*touching his forehead but putting his hand on his heart*) but I also know it here—where it hurts. Many and many a night I've been unable to sleep, thinking about it, feeling it—this hellish horror. So what can you tell me about it that I don't know and haven't felt already? Nothing—nothing—nothing. (*He moves down* L.C.)

DONNINGTON (*moving* R.). All right, all right. But you can't blame me for breaking out (*sits on the box down stage* R.) and damning and blasting the whole lunatic set-up, the hell on earth we've made and look like going on making. That's why I'm here—when I needn't have been—not because I'm patriotic—I can't swallow that gab, specially when its handed out to me by fellows who'd sell you anything and anybody for money, fellows who made it all stink for me before the war—no, I came out here—because—because——

JOSEPH (*firmly breaking in and crossing to* C.). You came out here to do your duty.

DONNINGTON. I didn't come out here to do my duty. I haven't any duty that brings me here. The world's not worth fighting for. We're a lot of blind maggots in a rotten carcase. I only came out here because if I'd stayed at home much longer, I'd have drunk myself paralytic——

JOSEPH. Well, why didn't you stay and drink yourself paralytic?

DONNINGTON. Trying to be funny?

JOSEPH. No. (*He goes up to the rock* R.C., *and sits*). You say that nothing matters, the world's not worth fighting for, and we're all a lot of blind maggots. Well, if that's true, what does

it matter if you stay at home—and lie and cheat and dodge and swindle—and drink yourself paralytic ?
DONNINGTON. Because I don't want to be that kind of chap.
JOSEPH. All right. You don't want to be that kind of chap. And all these horrors and miseries you talk so much about make you angry and despairing. They do something to you.
DONNINGTON. Of course they do something to me. They ought to do something to you too.
JOSEPH. Leave me out of it for a minute. But if they do something to you, and if you don't want to be that kind of chap, then you can't say nothing matters and there's no meaning in anything and that you're a blind maggot. Obviously there's something inside you—the something that gets angry or feels despair—that matters a lot. And what interests me isn't all that stuff you're talking, but that *something*. And it's that something I've been thinking about for some time now. I've been through all that, and now I'm coming out at the other end. (*He looks* L. *for a plane.*)
DONNINGTON. What other end ?
JOSEPH. Listen !

(*They listen carefully. Nothing can be heard yet.*)

DONNINGTON. Plane ?

(*Both men go on to the rostrum.*)

JOSEPH. Yes.

(*They stare* L., *through field-glasses.*)

DONNINGTON. One of ours, I think.
JOSEPH. Can't tell yet.
DONNINGTON. No, it isn't.
JOSEPH. One of theirs all right. Looks like the same plane that gunned us last night.

(*We now hear the plane distantly.*)

Here, we're taking no chances this time. (*Calling.*) Elvin ! Man the Bren ! Rest of you take cover !
ELVIN (*off* R.). Yers ?
JOSEPH (*calling*). Come on, Phil.

(*They hurry off* R. *The plane approaches and comes very low. But this time there is no machine-gunning. We hear the plane go away before we hear the men's voices. Then we hear the men off* R., *talking excitedly.* ELVIN *dashes on the stage and on to the rostrum.*)

HUGHES (*off*). Over there. I saw it distinctly.

(HUGHES *enters and moves up on the ramp, joining* ELVIN.)

SHAW (*entering, to* R.C.). I can't see owt.
ELVIN. No, 'e dropped something all right.
(JOSEPH *enters behind the tank and crosses to the rostrum* L., *followed by* DONNINGTON.)
Let Sar'n't Joseph 'ave a decco with his glasses. Look out, Taffy.
HUGHES. Over there, Sergeant. Look where I'm pointing.
JOSEPH. I know. I saw him drop it.
(SHAW *mounts the first ledge of rock,* L. *of the tank.*)
ELVIN. What's the idear ? Don't tell me ol' Jerry's started droppin' us a few eggs for breakfast.
DONNINGTON. Might be a little D.A. bomb.
JOSEPH. Doesn't look it to me.
ELVIN. Yer think it's the milk an' the mornin' pipers—see ? —and then when yer try to collect—up she goes.
SHAW. Let it alone, Ah say.
ELVIN (*turns to* HUGHES *and* SHAW). Remember them tins o' fags on the table in the Jerry camp ? Young Oosit—bloke with a squint Brum—makes a rush for 'em—an' the next minute 'is arm's gone—see ?
HUGHES. Up to every kind of dirty trick they are. Remember what the Engineer sergeant told us ?
ELVIN. Go on. I wouldn't listen to an Engineer sergeant if 'e told me my flamin' 'ouse was on fire.
JOSEPH (*after a pause*). I think it's a message of some sort. I'm going to get it.
DONNINGTON. Do you want anybody to come with you ?
JOSEPH (*handing his glasses to* DONNINGTON). No.
(*He hurries out* L. *The others watch him, throughout the following dialogue,* DONNINGTON *moving to* L. *end of the rocks.*)
ELVIN (*turns to* HUGHES *and* SHAW). There aren't many blokes with three tapes up that 'ud go an' do a job like that by themselves.
HUGHES. That is true. Sergeant Joseph will always take the risk himself.
ELVIN. That big-mouthed lance-jack who got 'imself transferred to 'edquarters—yer know the bloke I mean——
SHAW. Smithers.
ELVIN. That's right. Well, this big-mouthed Smithers says to me one time, 'e says, " That sar'n't o' yours is a teapot." So I says, " Well, what if 'e is ? " So 'e says, " Well, I don't like yids." So I says, " No, an' neither does 'Itler. Yer fighting on the wrong bloody side, cock."
DONNINGTON. Good for you, Knocker. (*He moves to the top ledge of the rock* L.C.)

ACT II]　　　DESERT HIGHWAY　　　55

ELVIN. Yids is like other people. There are good uns an' bad uns. But when they're good, they *are* good, see? Like Sergeant Joseph. So don't let's 'ear any more from you, Taffy.

HUGHES (*falling for it, indignantly*). From me? What do you mean—*from me*? Have I ever said one single word against Sergeant Joseph?

DONNINGTON. Button it. He's only pulling your leg.

(*He looks through his glasses while the others stare and wait.*)

SHAW. Sergeant's pickin' it up, isn't he?

DONNINGTON. Yes. He's taking the tin off the parachute now. If anything's going to happen, it'll happen now.

HUGHES. Making me sweat.

ELVIN. You'd sweat 'arder, chummie, if you was shakin' that tin can.

DONNINGTON. He's taking the top off.

SHAW. Steady. Nah—steady, lad.

DONNINGTON. He's found a piece of paper inside. He's looking at it. He's reading it. It must be a message.

ELVIN (*singing, looking at* HUGHES *and* SHAW).
　　"Inside it was a message,
　　With these words written on.
　　Whoever finds this bottle,
　　Finds the beer all gone."

DONNINGTON (*after a pause*). He's waving it. He's coming back.

(*He stops looking through the glasses, and sits down below the "idol." The others sit too, on the rostrum* C. *and* R.C.)

ELVIN. Four pints o' bitter an' can we 'ave the darts?

SHAW. Nay, don't start that, Knocker. It's bad enough without tormentin' ourselves.

DONNINGTON (*facetiously*). True for you, 'Erbert.

ELVIN. I'll bet they 'aven't got round to darts yet, up in Ossett.

SHAW. We used to 'ave a team at t'Are an' 'Ounds 'at 'ad beat onny team you Cockney lads could put up.

ELVIN (*mocking him*). "'Are an' 'Ounds!" Now, listen, Yorky——

DONNINGTON (*rather sharply*). Turn it up, Knocker. We might have to do a bit of thinking in a minute.

ELVIN. If yer goin' to do a bit o' thinkin' on the water question, yer can't start too soon.

SHAW. Ay, d'yer remember them three Recce Corps chaps they brought in after they'd bin lost? Ah—by gow—they couldn't talk—couldn't even swaller at first——

DONNINGTON (*sharply*). All right. We've got the idea.

SHAW. Well, Ah'm only sayin'.

DONNINGTON. All right. We know what you're saying and us don't want it. We happen to be lost too. Now keep quiet—this may be serious.

(*They look off expectantly, watching* JOSEPH *off* L. *After a few moments, he arrives* L. *hurriedly—hot, mopping himself, and carrying a piece of paper. He comes to* C., *below* ELVIN *and* HUGHES.)

(*Rising.*) It's a message, isn't it?

JOSEPH. Yes.

DONNINGTON (*moving to* L. *of* JOSEPH). In English?

JOSEPH. Near enough.

(*The others come down* R. *and* L. *of* JOSEPH, *forming a group.*)

SHAW. But that Jerry plane dropped it—eh?

JOSEPH. Yes. And this is what it says. (*He reads slowly and impressively.*) "Your armoured unit has retreated south-east. You are now cut off. If you will show white flag or any surrender token when we return this evening we will drop food and water in the morning to last until our panzer troops reach you in three or four days' time." Is that clear to everybody?

HUGHES. No, Sergeant, I'm a bit confused about it.

JOSEPH (*carefully*). According to them, we're completely cut off. They're coming back this way to-night. If we show them a white flag or any other sign that shows we're ready to surrender, then when they come this way in the morning they'll drop us enough food and water to last until we're captured.

DONNINGTON (*without any inflection*). And if we don't look as if we're surrendering——?

JOSEPH. They don't say anything about that. They might try bombing or machine-gunning us.

DONNINGTON. Or they might think it cheaper and easier to leave us here—to rot.

JOSEPH. Right.

ELVIN. 'Ere, 'alf a minute—'ow do we know them Jerries is tellin' the truth——?

JOSEPH. We don't know. Our chaps may not have retreated to the south-east at all, and we may not be completely cut off.

DONNINGTON. But we're not getting them on the wireless?

JOSEPH. No, we're not.

DONNINGTON. So they may have gone, and we may be cut off.

JOSEPH. Right. Well, there it is. (*Looking at them.*) You know everything I know.

(HUGHES *sits on the ledge* R.C.)

SHAW. 'Ow much water we got now?

ELVIN. Precious little real water. An' even that crawlin' green stuff along there's not goin' ter last more than another three days.

JOSEPH. True.

SHAW (*sitting on a low ledge of rock* R.). At that rate we'll 'ave our tongues 'anging out day after ter-morrer—same as them chaps——

ELVIN. Oh—turn it up! We know. They got us by the short 'airs. (*Leaning back against the rocks* C.)

(JOSEPH *moves down* R., *and turns to face them.*)

JOSEPH. Well, Phil, this is where the debate continues. You were telling me just before that plane came over and dropped its ultimatum that we were all a lot of fools and lunatics anyhow and that nothing mattered. It sounded just a lot of talk then—but now it isn't, you see. We've got to make a decision and act on it.

(ELVIN *and* HUGHES *rise.*)

DONNINGTON. You're asking me what I think we ought to do?

(ELVIN *faces* DONNINGTON.)

JOSEPH. Yes.

DONNINGTON. All right, then. I stick to what I said. I think we're a lot of fools to be here—and that nothing's going to get any better but probably worse——

JOSEPH. And so to-night we show a white flag—eh?

ELVIN (*angrily, turning to* JOSEPH). What?

DONNINGTON. No. Being a bloody fool and being here—I say—*no surrender.*

ELVIN (*bursting out*). An' I should think not. They'll get no bleedin' white flag out o' me—the murdering lyin' baskets.

JOSEPH. No surrender, eh?

(SHAW *rises.*)

DONNINGTON } (*together*). No.
ELVIN

JOSEPH. Shaw?

SHAW. Same 'ere.

JOSEPH. Hughes?

HUGHES. Certainly not indeed. I should feel ashamed for the rest of my life, and what's the use of living at all if you're going to feel ashamed all the time?

JOSEPH. No use. All right, boys. That's the way I thought you'd take it. Thanks.

DONNINGTON. But supposing we hadn't? Supposing we'd all been in favour of surrendering?

JOSEPH (*grimly, moving up to* C. *below the rostrum, facing up stage*). Then we'd have had another little war of our own, just here.

(DONNINGTON *sits*.)

Shaw, get back on the wireless again. See if that battery's woken up yet. One of us will relieve you in about half an hour. Keep on sending as well as listening.

SHAW (*going*). All right, Sergeant.

(*He goes off* R.)

JOSEPH. Better boil some of that well water, Knocker. And Hughes, bring the other gun out and we'll give it a good clean up. We may be wanting to use it soon.

HUGHES. Certainly, certainly.

(HUGHES *and* ELVIN *go off* R.)

DONNINGTON (*after a pause*). I never pretended to be consistent, y'know, Ben.

JOSEPH. No, you talk one way and act quite another way.

DONNINGTON But I'm still wondering what you meant when you said you'd been through all that and were now coming out at the other end You remember—I asked you "What other end?" And then we heard the plane. What did you mean?

JOSEPH (*slowly*). Well, you see, Phil—I'm a Jew.

DONNINGTON. You needn't bring that into it.

JOSEPH. I must.

DONNINGTON. But don't you see—if it's all going to turn on your being a Jew, then it's merely something special to you—and the other Jews—a few million at the most? And at the same time it's not going to mean anything to me—and the other fellows here—none of us Jews—and the thousand million other men who are wondering what it's all about.

JOSEPH. No. The way I see it, this means something to everybody. I'm only starting by explaining that I'm a Jew. Now this is very much our war isn't it?

DONNINGTON. It ought to be.

JOSEPH. It is.

(HUGHES *enters with the gun and stays down stage* R.)

You know what's been happening to the Jews? First, in Germany and Austria. Then in Czechoslovakia and Poland. And in the Nazi-occupied Ukraine, where old men, women, children have been packed into sealed trucks and gassed to death, where girls have been raped and then butchered, where children have been buried alive or had their brains bashed out. Every horror, every terror, every possible kind of mass murder,

To destroy the Jews, to blot us out altogether, to wipe us from the face of the earth.

(HUGHES *sits, near the box down* R.)

DONNINGTON. Yes, we know all about that. And it's mad and filthy. We're fighting to stop it.

JOSEPH. Even though nothing matters very much?

DONNINGTON. Don't harp on that. (*He moves over to* HUGHES R., *and spreads a ground sheet for the gun.*) Even though we live in a ridiculous and cruel world that never learns anything, some of us don't like madness and filth.

HUGHES. Quite right, Corporal. (*He places the tommy-gun on the ground sheet.*")

JOSEPH. Even if you don't know why?

DONNINGTON. Yes, even if we don't know why. (*He sits* L. *of* HUGHES.)

HUGHES. It isn't clean and decent. It's against everything we've been taught to believe. Though, mind you, Sergeant, with all due respect to you, I know people who don't like Jews and sometimes they seem to have good reasons.

DONNINGTON. Steady, Hughes.

JOSEPH. No, that's all right. I can understand that. We're a people who've had our wits sharpened—and sometimes been made unscrupulous—by hundreds of years of persecution and insecurity. A lot of our people behave rather badly. They're too sharp, too smart, make too much noise, are too pleased with themselves. But that's not what Hitler and the Nazis dislike about the Jews, nor why they want to destroy us. Their anti-Jewish madness is something quite different from ordinary prejudice.

DONNINGTON. I'll agree with that, Ben. But what is it they're after? Why do they invent all this fantastic nonsense about you Jews?

JOSEPH (*with growing urgency and force*). Because they want to destroy, once and for all, that idea which the two tribes of Judea have never quite lost—the idea of the great invisible Lord of Hosts, the one God of righteousness, to whom every man belongs, and to whom every man is precious and who should reign on earth, through man's free choice, as He reigns in Heaven.

DONNINGTON. And why should they want to do that?

JOSEPH (*passionately*). Because while that idea is still working in men's minds, the iron empires of fraud and force, of police and machines, of torture and murder, can never feel secure.

HUGHES (*fervently*). I agree with you, Sergeant—I do indeed. And, my word, you're quite a preacher.

DONNINGTON. That's the trouble, so far as I'm concerned. It sounds to me just like so much preaching—and that's all.

JOSEPH. That's all. But now we've got to start preaching. It's now or never.

DONNINGTON. But this religious stuff—it doesn't take with me. We're in a tough spot here. And I don't care about pie in the sky.

JOSEPH (*with force, moving down to* DONNINGTON). I'm not talking about pie in the sky. I'm talking about saving this world here and now, saving it from men's terrible destructiveness, passion, greed and fear.

DONNINGTON. That's more like it.

JOSEPH. But it's the same thing. Unless men believe that they belong to the eternal God of righteousness, who must have His Kingdom of compassion and fellowship and love here on earth, they'll destroy themselves and all they possess. (*He turns away* L. *a pace.*) Instead of *beauty*, there shall be burning. They won't go to some distant hell, they'll be in hell here.

DONNINGTON (*seriously*). I'll grant you that part. The hell on earth has started all right.

JOSEPH (*sitting on the ledge of rock* R.C.). Our great prophets once came striding out of these deserts to warn the kings and the rich men and the false priests that only the worship of the unseen God of righteousness would save the people from destruction. The ten tribes of the Northern Kingdom refused to listen to them, and then when the Assyrians—the Nazis of that time—mopped up the place and drove most of them to another part of the Assyrian Empire, these ten tribes completely disappeared, because they'd lost their identity.

DONNINGTON. The ten lost tribes, eh ? But what about the other two ?

JOSEPH. They never lost their identity, no matter what happened to them, because they never lost their sense of the one great invisible Lord God who was outside all the machinery of this world, who wasn't simply men's passions and lusts personified, or mere force, or the state. And the Nazis and all the people like them who are trying to destroy us are doing it because they're trying to destroy any hold that idea has on men's minds, so that they can turn people into blind, unthinking, unfeeling masses—sleepwalkers, robots, slaves of the machines. And *that's* what we're fighting.

DONNINGTON. That's what we may be fighting against. But what are we fighting for ? The Bank of England and the Federation of British Industries and Carlton Club democracy ?

JOSEPH. No, we're fighting for the real democracy, which is something more than having an occasional vote. It's the belief that all human beings are precious to God, and that therefore all human beings must be precious to each other, and that the will of God shall be done on earth as it is in heaven.

ACT II] DESERT HIGHWAY 61

DONNINGTON (*with mocking gesture at the desert*). It looks like it, doesn't it?
JOSEPH (*quoting emphatically*). " Make straight in the desert a highway for our God."
HUGHES (*quoting with enthusiasm*). " And the ransomed of the Lord shall return, and come to Zion with songs and everlasting joy upon their heads! they shall obtain joy and gladness, and sorrow and sighing shall flee away."
(ELVIN *enters* R., *above the tank, quietly, and stands between* DONNINGTON *and* HUGHES.)
ELVIN. An' everythink in the garden's luvly. But when does all this start 'appenin'?
JOSEPH (*firmly*). It starts happening when we trust in the strength of God—and *make it happen*.
ELVIN (*moving to* R. *of* JOSEPH). Well, I oughta warn yer, Sergeant, that by this time, termorrer, we'll 'ave abaht a mug o' water each—an' then finish.
JOSEPH (*fiercely*). All right, Knocker. (*He rises, moves up to the ledge* L.C., *and picks up the Bible.*)
ELVIN (*to* C.). An' that don't mean I'm suggestin' any bleedin' white flags o' surrender neither.
JOSEPH (*turning to face* ELVIN, *from* L.C.). All right, all right. We'll start cutting the water down to the very minimum to-day. And don't forget I've got those two tins of fruit. They'll help us out a bit.
DONNINGTON. I've got a tin too that goes into the kitty.
ELVIN (*turning to* HUGHES). Well, Taffy, yer better make up yer mind to get yer everlastin' joy an' gladness out o' your share o' three tins o' fruit an' 'alf a mug o' slimy water. (*To them all, moving up to the edge of the rocks, a little* R. *of* C.) But what is all this, any'ow? Beveridge Report? League o' Nations? Or 'ave yer got religion?
JOSEPH (*in ringing confident tone*). It's all three, Knocker. It's our hope, our future, our life. (*A pace or two down* L.C.) About twenty-six hundred years ago, which was a time rather like this, with huge armies on the move and cities burning, from the desert not a long way from here there came a prophet called Micah the Morasthite. And he had listened to the voice from the heart of the silence, and has seen visions in the darkness of the night. It's all here in this Bible that belonged to George Wick—(*he reads in title-page, quietly*) " Georgie, from his loving Mother on his eighteenth birthday——"
ELVIN (*uneasily*). Take it easy, Sergeant. I was terrible fond o' young Georgie. (*He sits on the ledge* R.C., *facing* HUGHES.)
JOSEPH (*quietly, sitting on the corner of the rostrum,* L. *of* C.). I'm not trying to rub it in. I'm trying to put it out. He died for something, not for nothing. And this is what the prophet

Micah said to the unhappy people of that time, and what he's still saying to us. (*He reads quietly.*) " But in the last days it shall come to pass that the mountain of the house of the Lord shall be established in the top of the mountains, and it shall be exalted above the hills ; and people shall flow unto it.

" And the Lord shall judge among many people, and rebuke strong nations afar off ; and they shall beat their swords into plowshares, and their spears into pruninghooks ; nation shall not lift up a sword against nation, neither shall they learn war any more.

" But they shall sit every man under his vine and under his fig tree ; and none shall make them afraid ; for the mouth of the Lord of Hosts hath spoken it. For all people will walk every one in the name of his god, and we will walk in the name of the Lord our God for ever and ever."

HUGHES (*seriously*). Amen !

ELVIN. Well, I don't know. If you'll change that vine an' fig trees—'cos I don't want to sit under any bleedin' vine an' fig trees—but if yer change that for sittin' in the Royal Oak or the Red Lion—I'll say Amen too.

(*Enter* SHAW *from* R.)

SHAW. Sergeant, Sergeant ! there's some life in that battery. Ah can 'car something—but Ah can't make out what it is yet.

DONNINGTON (*holding up his head*). Wait a minute. I can hear something too ! Listen !

JOSEPH. It's a plane.

(*As they listen, we can just hear it in the distance. Gradually they turn their heads and look up in the same direction.*)

DONNINGTON. It's a plane all right.

JOSEPH. But—ours or theirs ?

The plane is nearer and they are still staring as—

The CURTAIN *slowly comes down.*

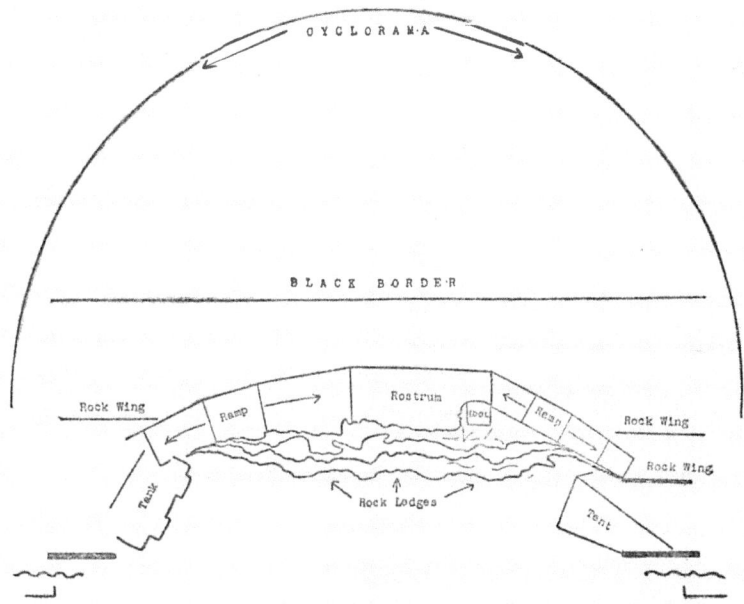

PROPERTY PLOT

ACT I

Covering stage.—Half a yard of fine sand.
Down stage, L.—Tent (as shown in Ground Plan) with sandbags on bases for stability.
In tent.—First-aid box. 1 enamelled mug.
On stage L.C. (*above tent*). 1 petrol-can.
Above low ledge of rock L.C.—A carved stone, effigy, or idol, set in a socket. (Repeated in Act II.)
Below, and to L. *of "idol."*—1 petrol-can
On stage, L.C.—A mound of sand, a sandbag partly filled, and a shovel.
On stage, down R.—1 beer box. Above it, and to L., another partly filled sandbag, and 3 empty sandbags.
On stage R., *below* R. *end of ramp.*—An army tank. (Grant pattern.) This may be partially hidden by proscenium. There must be space above and below it for exit.
On tank.—Tarpaulin. 2 Army rugs. Camouflage net.
On rock (*at the back*, R.C.).—1 rug.
On stage, behind rocks.—5 rat traps set for machine-gun effect.
  (*For lay-out of ramps, rostrum, and rock ledges, see Ground Plan.*)

OFF STAGE (L. *side*)

Long gun box (empty).
Large dixie of tea, with milk and sugar.
Small dixie of two tins of vegetable soup, cube of Oxo, and bread.
6 small dixie tins.
5 enamelled mugs.
5 spoons.
1 fork.
Ground-sheet.
Tommy-gun.

Note.—If the "tank" is not possible, rocks similar to those in the Interlude, but lower, may be set, with the top of a "tank" visible behind them

INTERLUDE

Strike tank, tent, and all modern Army properties.
Replace worn "idol" with its counterpart, less "worn."
Rock piece R., in place of tank.
In place of tent L., set 4 tea-chests covered with felt and hessian (or canvas) bound up as packages.
Another, a little farther on stage, with bindings loose, and a large coloured blanket rolled up and bound.
Another long blanket, rolled, off L.
2 small bundles (one smaller than the other) down R.

ACT II

Stage properties as at the end of Act I.
(Tank, tent, and "worn" idol replaced.)
A filled sandbag by the wheel of the tank.
A cape folded, on the top of the tank.
Gun on ground-sheet (C.).
Gun off stage, L.
In tent.—1 rug.
  WICK'S Bible, paybook, papers, etc.

COSTUME PLOT

ACT I

JOSEPH : Set of black overalls with stripes on R. arm only. Black boots. Coloured scarf round neck. Black R.T.C. beret with badge. Webbing belt with ·38 pistol in holster attached to a lanyard, worn round the neck.

DONNINGTON : Long drill slacks. Desert boots. Officer's shirt. Coloured pullover tucked inside slacks. Coloured handkerchief round neck. Webbing belt. R.T.C. beret, pistol and holster similar to JOSEPH'S.

ELVIN : Set of dirty brown overalls. Ammunition boots. Webbing belt and pistol. R.T.C. beret. Old scarf round neck.

HUGHES : Drill shorts. Drill Bush shirt. Socks rolled down over ammunition boots. R.T.C. beret, webbing belt, and pistol.

SHAW : Long drill slacks. Drill Bush shirt. Leather jerkin. Ammunition boots. Leather belt. (*NO* pistol.)

WICK : Drill shorts. "Issue" pullover. Ammunition boots. Socks. Belt and pistol.

(*No changes in the above for Act II.*)

INTERLUDE

JOSEPH : Black, shabby, and dirty-looking robes to below knees. High black hat with sun-flap at back—so that no hair is visible. Brown sandals. Full black beard and moustache.

DONNINGTON : White robes to ankles (very clean and flowing). Gold collar and belt. Silver and gold bangles. Brown and white striped hat reaching to below neck at the back. Brown sandals.

ELVIN : Grey-blue short-sleeved tunic. Light colour long slacks—baggy. Coloured sash. Black semi-skullcap. Brown sandals. Full red beard and moustache.

HUGHES : Long tunic to ground. Over-cape with wide sleeves. Yellow and brown sash. Semi-skullcap with sun-flap. Brown sandals. Thin black beard and moustache.

SHAW : Tunic, etc., as for HUGHES. High hat with red stripes. Brown sandals. Short half-brown beard.

WICK : Loin cloth. Gay coloured vest. Turban type hat. Sandals.

LIGHTING PLOT

ACT I

To Open.—*Floats :* Blue full, amber ¾, pink ½, white *nil.*
No. 1 *Batten :* Blue full, amber full, pink ¾, white *nil.*
No. 2 *Batten :* Ditto.
No. 3 *Batten :* Blue full, amber ½, pink and white *nil.*
No. 4 *Batten and/or flood bar on top of cyclorama :* No. 20 blue.
Stage Floods on cyclorama : No. 18 blue, frost.
Ground Row on cyclorama : Amber and blue at ½.
F.O.H. (or Perches) : Flood No. 4 amber, frost.

Cue 1.—DONNINGTON. " I hope the kid's all right, but I have a feeling he isn't " : Commence slow check of all amber in floats, ground row, battens, and F.O.H. (about 3 minutes).

Cue 2.—DONNINGTON. " All right, Knocker." (*Exit* ELVIN L.) : Check down all pinks in floats and battens, slowly to *nil.* Change flood on cyclorama to No. 20, bringing in No. 12 spot, frost, slowly, on L. lower edge of cyclorama. Fade out F.O.H. amber, at the same time fading in R. perch No. 16 blue on L.C. acting area on and around the " idol " very slowly.

Cue 3.—SHAW. " I might ha' one or two ideas of my own " : Slightly focus R. perch spot around " idol." Check down blues in floats and battens by ½. No. 12 spot L. cyclorama now up and remains until next cue.

Cue 4.—JOSEPH *moves to the tent, followed by* DONNINGTON : Fade No. 12 spot on cyclorama. Commence fade-out of all blues in floats and battens, to complete just before the CURTAIN. Ditto for ground row on cyclorama, but rather quicker. Ditto for stage floods on cyclorama ; No. 4 battens and/or flood bar on top of cyclorama remain, checked a little, at CURTAIN fall.

Cue 5.—SHAW. " Thousands of years . . ." : All blues (except No. 4 batten) are out. L. perch on " idol " fades slowly and stage flood (or ground row) on bottom of cyclorama fades in, No. 16, as the CURTAIN falls.

INTERLUDE AND ACT II

Floats and Nos. 1, 2 *and* 3 *Battens :* Amber and pink FULL, white ¾.
No. 4 *Batten :* Blue full.
Flood Bar on top of cyclorama : No. 18 blue.
Flood on cyclorama : Steel.
Ground Row : Amber and white ½, blue ¼.
F.O.H. (or Perches) : Flood stage straw.
No Cues.

www.ingramcontent.com/pod-product-compliance
Ingram Content Group UK Ltd.
Pitfield, Milton Keynes, MK11 3LW, UK
UKHW021917060225
454771UK00026B/637